MW00657397

A Teenager's Guide to

Healthy Relationships

Scriptural Secrets for Building
Satisfying and Successful Relationships

To order additional copies:

www.stayinthecastle.com

or call (812) 665-4375

All Scripture from the King James Bible

Printed in the United States of America

A Teenager's Guide to

Healthy Relationships

Scriptural Secrets for Building
Satisfying and Successful Relationships

by Jerry Ross

Other Books by the Author

Seven Royal Laws of Courtship
The Teenage Years of Jesus Christ
The Childhood Years of Jesus Christ
The 21 Tenets of Biblical Femininity
The 21 Tenets of Biblical Masculinity
Is Your Youth Group Dead or Alive?
Mountain Lessons
Grace Will Lead Me Home
104 Teen Bible Lessons
Did God Put a Book Inside of You?

Stay in the Castle Series

Stay in the Castle
The Warrior Prince
The Chosen One
The Prodigals

The Teenager's Guide Series

A Teenager's Guide to Character, Success, & Happiness
A Teenager's Guide to the Invisible Creation
A Teenager's Guide to Healthy Relationships

Ultimate Goal Publications

Order by phone or online

(812) 665-4375

www.stayinthecastle.com

Table of Contents

Dedicated to my wife, Sheryl,

For all you do and all you are.

Introduction

The Secret to Successful Relationships

A drastic shift occurred in America's dialogue half way through the last century. For much of the first 200 years of our nation's history, the buzz phrase touted by politicians, principals and parents was "civic responsibility." As a result, generations of American citizens grew up understanding that each had a moral obligation to identify and fulfill their personal and public responsibilities by stepping up and paying forward all that others had invested in them.

Then suddenly, the buzz phrase changed. No one was talking about civic responsibilities. Instead, everyone was talking about civil rights. As a result, our nation changed. People stopped considering what they owed, and instead became focused on what they perceived they were owed. Rights replaced responsibility and a nation of victors became a nation of victims.

As a result, not only did our country change, but our personal relationships began to change. You see, what made us successful as a nation is the same thing that made us successful as spouses, as parents, as employees, as brothers and sisters, as friends, and as citizens. When we traded in our responsibilities for our rights, we poisoned every human and divine relationship available to us.

What is the secret ingredient to a successful relationship? One word: responsibility. In the chapters ahead, we will identify the wonderful relationships available to us, and then consider from God's Word the responsibilities attached to each relationship. By doing so, I hope to change your thinking. If that occurs, it will also change your life and maybe, just maybe, we can get our nation back.

-1-

America's Fastest Growing Religion

Lesson Goals:

1. To understand the root sin that will produce all other last day sins.
2. To understand how self-love can become self-worship.
3. To understand how to Biblically prioritize our love.

What is the fastest growing religion in America today? Well, my internet search produced a list of confusing statistics mingled with authoritative claims. The Mormons claim it is Mormonism, while the Jehovah's Witnesses argue for themselves. Most statistics point to Islam, although several articles touted the number one new belief is unbelief — giving the title to Atheism.

I am going to contend that it is none of these. Based on my 57 years of life and 30 plus years of ministry experience, I can tell you what it is — and there isn't even a close second.

The fastest growing religion in America today is the religion of self-worship.

The Religion of Self-Worship

2 Timothy 3:1-5, "*This know also, that in the last days perilous times shall come.* ***For men shall be lovers of their own selves,*** *covetous, boasters, proud, blasphemers, disobedient to parents, unthankful, unholy, Without natural affection, trucebreakers, false accusers, incontinent, fierce, despisers of those that are good, Traitors, heady, highminded, lovers of pleasures more than lovers* *of God; Having a form of godliness, but denying the power thereof: from such turn away."*

The wild growth of the religion of self-worship was predicted in the Scriptures. It is the inevitable result of the first sin of the last days — the sin of self-love. I believe that all sins listed after self-love, in the above passage, stem from the first one.

God knew that the natural inclination of fallen man would be to love themselves first. When God delivered the first and second great commandments, His highest expectation for us loving our neighbors is revealed in the second command.

Matthew 22:36-39, *"Master, which is the great commandment in the law? Jesus said unto him, Thou shalt love the Lord thy God with all thy heart, and with all thy soul, and with all thy mind. This is the first and great commandment. And the second is like unto it, Thou shalt love thy neighbour as thyself."*

It's kind of pathetic when you think about it. God knows that men are so strongly inclined to love themselves that God set the bar of loving others to this standard: Love your neighbor as much as you do yourselves.

Notice the wording in God's admonition to husbands urging them to love their wives in these verses:

Ephesians 5:28-33, *"So ought men to love their wives as their own bodies. He that loveth his wife loveth himself. For no man ever yet hated his own flesh; but nourisheth and cherisheth it, even as the Lord the church... Nevertheless let every one of you in particular so love his wife even as himself; and the wife see that she reverence her husband."*

Again, it's pretty sad that the best God seems to be able to expect from men when it comes to loving their wives is a love equal to their own self-love.

Romans 1:22-25, *"Professing themselves to be wise, they became fools, And changed the glory of the un-*

corruptible God into an image made like to corruptible man, and to birds, and fourfooted beasts, and creeping things. Wherefore God also gave them up to uncleanness through the lusts of their own hearts, to dishonour their own bodies between themselves: Who changed the truth of God into a lie, ***and worshipped and served the creature more than the Creator,*** *who is blessed for ever. Amen."*

Today, self-love has mutated into self-worship. This reprobate society has fulfilled the prophecy found in Romans chapter one, for we now have "...worshipped and served the creature more than the Creator."

Whitney Houston, the multi-platinum American singer, notched a mega-hit when she sang "The Greatest Love of All." Since Ms. Houston grew up singing in the church choir, one might fairly assume this song to be about God's love for us, or maybe our love for Him. But no — the words instead promoted the new religion of self-worship.

Because the greatest

Love of all is happening to me,

I found the greatest

Love of all inside of me.

The greatest love of all,

Is easy to achieve,

Learning to love yourself,

It is the greatest love of all.

Did this self-love philosophy of life translate into a personal life of happiness and joy for Ms. Houston? Although we cannot know all that was in her heart, her life tells a story. Public fame did not keep her from a private life of drug abuse. On February 11, 2012, Whitney Houston was found unconscious in her suite at the Beverly

Hilton Hotel, submerged in her bathtub. The Los Angeles County Coroner's Office later reported that Houston's death was caused by drowning and "the effects of atherosclerotic heart disease and cocaine use." She was only 48 years of age.

An interesting side note to her sad ending: on February 9, 2012, Whitney made her last public performance when she joined Kelly Price on stage in Hollywood, California, and sang "Jesus Loves Me." Two days later, she died.

Never forget, the greatest love of all is the love God showed to us when He sent Jesus to die for us. And the greatest love we are capable of is, first, a love for God, and second, to love our neighbors as ourselves. These two loves — not self-love — bring the greatest joy of all.

Self-love has been so promoted and defended in our society, so ingrained in our psyche, that even Christians seem to recoil at the notion of self-denial. I am sure Jesus Christ shocked some of His followers when He spoke of the subject of discipleship.

Matthew 16:24-25, *"Then said Jesus unto his disciples, If any man will come after me, let him deny himself, and take up his cross, and follow me. For whosoever will save his life shall lose it: and whosoever will lose his life for my sake shall find it."*

The self-love and self-worship that permeates the church has all but eliminated the pool of Christians from which God calls His disciples. Deny oneself? What a foreign concept for many today.

Andrew Murray said, "A true revival means nothing less than a revolution, casting out the spirit of worldliness and selfishness, and making God and His love triumph in the heart and life."

Thomas à Kempis wrote, "Let this be thy whole endeavor, this thy prayer, this thy desire, that thou mayest be stripped of all selfishness, and with entire simplicity follow Jesus only."

By now, you are asking, "Preacher, what does this have to do with healthy relationships?" Everything.

If you missed my rant in the book's introduction about rights versus responsibilities, go back and read it. You will never foster proper relationships when you are more worried about your rights than you are your responsibilities. If you gauge the success of a relationship on what the other person does or does not do for you, then you are setting yourself up for constant disappointments. But if you are willing to study and understand YOUR responsibilities in each relationship, and work hard to fulfill them, then you can build lasting and fulfilling ties to those around you.

Nothing will destroy your relationships faster than self-love and self-worship. It is hard to love others when most all your love is already reserved for yourself. Self-denial increases your ability to invest properly and responsibly in those around you. The more you love God and people, and the more you can deny yourself, the more healthy your relationships will become. And believe it or not, the happier you will be.

We teach the children who attend our church a simple, saintly song. It contains the secret to both healthy relationships and a happy life.

"Jesus and others and you,
What a wonderful way to spell JOY.
Jesus and others and you,
In the life of each girl and each boy.
*J is for Jesus for He has **first place**,*
*O is for **others** you meet face to face.*
Y is for you and whatever you do,
*So put yourself **third** and spell JOY."*

Paul, perhaps the greatest apostle of all, wrote, *"I die daily," I Corinthians 15:31.* His love was spent on God first, then lost souls and his Christian brothers and sisters. He achieved great things because he decided to start each day dying to self. What an example!

Want successful relationships? Want to impact people for the cause of Christ? Want to live a life that really means something for eternity? Then forget about you and spend your life living for God and living for others.

Points to Ponder and Discuss:

1. What is the difference between rights and responsibilities?

2. Why is self-love a hindrance to every other relationship available to us?

3. Can self-love eventually mutate into self-worship? How?

-2-

Your Relationship to Jesus (Part 1)

Lesson Goals:

1. To learn of the price Jesus paid to have a relationship with us.

2. To understand how we can access this relationship.

3. To learn how all other relationships are affected by our relationship with Jesus Christ.

The Most Important of All Relationships

Not everyone who lives out their lives on this earth will enjoy a marriage relationship. Not all will know what it is to be called "Daddy" or "Mommy." Some, sadly, may go through life and never experience what it is to have a close, personal friendship with another human being. Some have never met their grandparents, or might never get to meet their grandchildren.

But the MOST IMPORTANT of all relationships is available to each and every person who has ever been granted life on this earth. It is a "whosoever" relationship offered to all.

John 3:14-17, *"And as Moses lifted up the serpent in the wilderness, even so must the Son of man be lifted up: That whosoever believeth in him should not perish, but have eternal life. For God so loved the world, that he gave his only begotten Son, that whosoever believeth in him should not perish, but have everlasting life. For God sent not his Son into the world to condemn the world; but that the world through him might be saved."*

Romans 10:9-13, *"That if thou shalt confess with thy mouth the Lord Jesus, and shalt believe in thine heart that God hath raised him from the dead, thou shalt be saved. For with the heart man believeth unto righteousness; and with the mouth confession is made unto salvation... For whosoever shall call upon the name of the Lord shall be saved."*

The relationship offered to every one of us is the relationship we can have with Jesus Christ as our Savior. Of all the relationships of life, this is the most important because it determines our eternal destination.

What Destroyed Our Relationship With God?

At one time, mankind had a wonderful and sweet relationship with God. God created a man and a woman, placed them in a beautiful garden paradise, and fellowshipped with them each evening, walking beside them in the cool of the day. God gave them everything they could have desired. He had but one restriction — one rule. They were not to eat of the tree of the knowledge of good and evil.

Genesis 2:16-17, *"And the LORD God commanded the man, saying, Of every tree of the garden thou mayest freely eat: But of the tree of the knowledge of good and evil, thou shalt not eat of it: for in the day that thou eatest thereof thou shalt surely die."*

Notice the penalty attached to the "thou shalt not." If they chose to disobey the Lord and eat fruit from the forbidden tree, then the penalty was death. For a time, the man and woman heeded God's warning and enjoyed God's fellowship, but then came the day that the Devil came to tempt them.

Genesis 3:4-11, *"And the serpent said unto the woman, Ye shall not surely die: For God doth know that in the day ye eat thereof, then your eyes shall be opened, and ye shall be as gods, knowing good and evil. And when the woman saw that the tree was good for food, and that it* *was pleasant to the eyes, and a tree to be desired to make one wise, she took of the fruit thereof, and did eat, and gave also unto her husband with her; and he did eat. And the eyes of them both were opened, and they knew that they were naked; and they sewed fig leaves together, and made themselves aprons. And the LORD God called unto Adam, and said unto him, Where art thou? And he said, I heard thy voice in the garden, and I was afraid, because I was naked; and I hid myself. And he said, Who told thee that thou wast naked? Hast thou eaten of the tree, whereof I commanded thee that thou shouldest not eat?"*

What destroyed the relationship God had with mankind? The answer is disobedience to God by breaking a law of God. In short, ***sin*** destroyed our relationship with a holy God.

1 John 3:4, *"Whosoever committeth sin transgresseth also the law: for sin is the transgression of the law."*

Romans 3:23, *"For all have sinned, and come short of the glory of God;"*

Romans 6:23, *"For the wages of sin is death...*

James 2:10, *"For whosoever shall keep the whole law, and yet offend in one point, he is guilty of all."*

Well, as you can see, our sin has left us in a mess! We cannot throw stones at Adam and Eve, because we all have made the same choice. We all have sinned, and by doing so, we are all guilty before God and unfit for Heaven. Left in this state, without someone to save us from our sinfulness, we are doomed to an eternity separated from God in a horrible, wicked place we were never intended to go.

Matthew 25:41, *"Then shall he say also unto them on the left hand, Depart from me, ye cursed, into everlasting fire, prepared for the devil and his angels:"*

Revelation 21:8, *"But the fearful, and unbelieving, and the abominable, and murderers, and whoremongers, and sorcerers, and idolaters, and all liars, shall have their* *part in the lake which burneth with fire and brimstone: which is the second death."*

Revelation 20:11-15, *"And I saw a great white throne, and him that sat on it, from whose face the earth and the heaven fled away; and there was found no place for them. And I saw the dead, small and great, stand before God; and the books were opened: and another book was opened, which is the book of life... And whosoever was not found written in the book of life was cast into the lake of fire."*

Mankind Needed a Savior!

Sin had left us guilty, hopeless and doomed. If God chose to do nothing, our fate was sealed. But then came the Gospel — the good news! God loved us even though we pretty much messed up everything. And He had a plan to send us a Savior.

Luke 2:11, *"For unto you is born this day in the city of David a Saviour, which is Christ the Lord."*

John 4:42, *"And said unto the woman, Now we believe, not because of thy saying: for we have heard him ourselves, and know that this is indeed the Christ, the Saviour of the world."*

1 John 4:14, *"And we have seen and do testify that the Father sent the Son to be the Saviour of the world."*

Titus 3:5-6, *"Not by works of righteousness which we have done, but according to his mercy he saved us, by the washing of regeneration, and renewing of the Holy Ghost; Which he shed on us abundantly through Jesus Christ our Saviour;"*

Jesus was sent by God to be the Savior of the world! Someone had to save us from our sin and from the penalty of our sin. We needed both forgiveness and deliverance. Jesus Christ came to earth and provided both! And the way He did it is known as the Gospel story.

The Gospel Story

Romans 1:16, *"For I am not ashamed of the gospel of Christ: for it is the power of God unto salvation to every one that believeth; to the Jew first, and also to the Greek."*

1 Corinthians 15:1-4, *"Moreover, brethren, I declare unto you the gospel which I preached unto you, which also ye have received, and wherein ye stand; By which also ye are saved, if ye keep in memory what I preached unto you, unless ye have believed in vain. For I delivered unto you first of all that which I also received, how that Christ died for our sins according to the scriptures; And that he was buried, and that he rose again the third day according to the scriptures:"*

Jesus, God's Son, came into the world as a babe born to a virgin young lady. He lived a sinless life, and by doing so, did not need to die for His own sins. Instead, He chose to die for our sins. Here is the good news: He took our place! He took our punishment! He paid the penalty of our sin! And He offers to all both forgiveness and deliverance.

What is Your Responsibility in This Relationship?

Is Jesus Christ your Savior? He wants to be. What is required to receive God's forgiveness and be saved from Hell? Just two things: you must know how badly you need it, and you must be willing to receive it.

Acts 16:29-31, *"Then he called for a light, and sprang in, and came trembling, and fell down before Paul and Silas, And brought them out, and said, Sirs, what must I do to be saved? And they said, Believe on the Lord Jesus Christ, and thou shalt be saved, and thy house."*

John 1:11-12, *"He came unto his own, and his own received him not. But as many as received him, to them gave he power to become the sons of God, even to them that believe on his name:"*

Jesus paid it all! You cannot pay for your sins, and you cannot be good enough to earn Heaven. There is nothing for you to do except trust in what Jesus has already done.

Jesus wants to be your Savior. If God is dealing with your heart, and He has brought you to the point where you know that you are a sinner, and you are under conviction about your sin, then you can be saved right now. You must believe that Jesus died for your sins, was buried and rose again. And you must receive Jesus Christ as your personal Savior. You do this by calling upon Him in prayer, and asking Him to forgive you and to save you.

Romans 10:13, *"For whosoever shall call upon the name of the Lord shall be saved."*

The most important relationship you can have is knowing Jesus Christ as your Savior. If you are not saved, my prayer is that you will be saved right now. If you are saved, consider this: where would we be right now if Jesus had been more concerned with His rights than His responsibilities? Christ put our needs above His. He loved us — not as much as Himself — but much more than Himself. By doing this He set before us the greatest example of what it takes to have a proper relationship. Now, let's offer the same to those around us.

Let's be like Jesus.

Points to Ponder and Discuss

Ponder the sweet message of salvation. Have you accepted Jesus Christ as your Savior? If not, why not now?

-3-

Your Relationship to Jesus (Part 2)

Lesson Goals

1. To understand Christ's desire to be our friend.

2 To understand our responsibilities in this relationship.

After you receive Jesus as your Savior, the depth of this new relationship is still unmined. Jesus does not just want to be your Savior, He wants to be so much more. He wants to be your very best friend.

"Who is Your Best Friend?"

The church in which I was saved as a child had a wonderful pastor's wife. Her name was Mrs. Vietta Evans. Every Wednesday evening, she would herd us children out of the auditorium and into a classroom to teach us Bible stories. Mrs. Evans was a master story teller, and gifted in keeping our attention.

One Wednesday, after getting us properly seated and arranged, she started the class by asking us a question.

"Tonight, I want you each to tell me the name of your very best friend." Eyes darted around the room as we each thought over our list of classmates and chums. Then, she called upon each of us to speak a name, and after the last of us had spoken, she became visibly distraught.

"I need to apologize to each of you! I have done a terrible job as your Bible teacher! My, how I've failed you!"

Immediately we were all a bit anxious. Somehow, we knew we had failed in our answers but none of us could figure out why. Finally she looked at us, eyes brimming with tears, and said, "I can't believe that none of you said, 'Jesus'."

I was only six years old when that happened, but it has stuck with me all these years. Why shouldn't that be the immediate answer of every Christian? Why isn't Jesus our best friend? What stands in the way of this most blessed of all relationships?

How to Build a Lasting Friendship with Christ

1. Realize that Jesus has already proven His friendship toward you. To understand this, you must develop a Biblical view of what true friendship really is.

Jesus has proved His friendship by loving you unconditionally. *A friend loveth at all times... Proverbs 17:17.* As a child of God, there is nothing that can separate you from the love of Christ. Sometimes that is hard for a teenager to really believe, especially in this world of broken homes and broken lives. Some of you have been disappointed by those who at one time claimed to love you, but then later turned their backs on you. Jesus is a true friend — He loves you at all times. I'm not saying that Christ is not disappointed in you at times, but I am saying that He never stops loving you.

The ultimate test of undying friendship is the willingness to die. Jesus proved His love to you by making the ultimate sacrifice for you. *"Greater love hath no man than this, that a man lay down his life for his friends." John 15:13.*

2. Jesus offers His friendship to every teenager. One of the most remarkable things we learn about God is that He has, in the past, developed personal friendships with men.

God called Abraham His friend (Exodus 33:11, II Chronicles 20:7, Isaiah 41:8, James 2:23). The Bible tells us that God spoke to Moses, "as a man speaketh unto his friend," (Exodus 33:11). David had such a close personal relationship with God that God described him as a "man after mine own heart," (Acts 13:22).

God is no respecter of persons. He will not offer to one what He will not make available to all!

Acts 10:34-35, *"Then Peter opened his mouth, and said, Of a truth I perceive that God is no respecter of persons: But in every nation he that feareth him, and worketh righteousness, is accepted with him."*

God the Son affirms his desire to befriend you. Jesus Christ wants to be your best friend.

John 15:15, *"Henceforth I call you not servants; for the servant knoweth not what his lord doeth: but I have called you friends; for all things that I have heard of my Father I have made known unto you."*

Jesus did not just wish to enlist disciples to help Him reach the world, He sought friends to walk beside Him. "I have called you friends!" What a wonderful thing for Christ to desire to befriend someone like me!

3. No matter what you have done, Jesus still offers to you friendship. I have counseled enough teenagers to know that the Devil has convinced many today that God does not love them and certainly does not want to be their friend. I've had young people look at me and say, "Preacher, if you knew what I have done, and who I really am, you would not want me in your church." Another said, "I understand that God loves the other teens in the church, but God could never love and forgive me. I've just gone too far."

What they fail to understand is that once Jesus saves you, He will never forsake you. In that regard, He is your best friend. *"Thine own friend, and thy father's friend, forsake not..." Proverbs 27:10.*

Hebrews 13:5, *"Let your conversation be without covetousness; and be content with such things as ye have: for he hath said, I will never leave thee, nor forsake thee."*

Still not convinced? Think you are just too bad? One of Jesus' trusted disciples betrayed Him — sold Him out for 40 pieces of silver! Then he had the audacity to betray Him with a kiss! Notice the words of Jesus:

Matthew 26:48-50, *"Now he that betrayed him gave them a sign, saying, Whomsoever I shall kiss, that same is he: hold him fast. And forthwith he came to Jesus and said, Hail, master; and kissed him. And Jesus said unto him,* ***Friend,*** *wherefore art thou come? Then came they, and laid hands on Jesus, and took him."*

Guess what? Jesus already understands that you are not perfect. He understands that you will often fail. But that is not the basis of your friendship with Him. He is your friend because He has decided to be your friend. And He doesn't forsake His friends!

Proverbs 16:28, *"...a whisperer separateth chief friends."*

Some teens think they have sinned away the opportunity to be Christ's friend. A "whisperer" (Satan!) has been putting these thoughts in their minds. The Devil is the "accuser of the brethren" and he spends much of his time trying to throw our sin back in our faces. Maybe there is something in your past that the Devil won't let you forget. If you have taken it to the Lord and sought forgiveness, then God has not only forgiven it, but forgotten it!

My dad used to tell me, "When the Devil wants to remind you of your past, remind him of his future!"

***1 John 1:9**, "If we confess our sins, he is faithful and just to forgive us our sins, and to cleanse us from all unrighteousness."*

4. A real friend tells you what you need to hear, even if it is sometimes not what you want to hear.

***Proverbs 27:6**, "Faithful are the wounds of a friend; but the kisses of the enemy are deceitful.*

One of the true tests of friendship is complete honesty. Jesus once again proves to us His desire to be our friend by always being honest with us. He is the "Word" that was made flesh and dwelt among us. The Bible will always be straightforward with you, and will always tell you the truth.

Many times, teens mistake flattery for friendship. Someone comes into their lives and begins to tell them things they want to hear – to flatter their pride or encourage their disobedience and rebellion. This person is not their friend. Jesus will always tell you the truth, even when it hurts! He does this for our good.

Your pastor — who preaches the truth — is your friend. Your parents, who love you enough to be honest with you, are some of the dearest friends you will ever have. Don't wait till you are in your 30s or 40s to appreciate your dad and mom.

5. If you want to be a friend to Jesus, you need to show yourself friendly.

Much of what we have taught thus far was to convince you that Jesus Christ is a friend worth having! The Bible has shown us that He proves to us every day how much He loves us and how much He desires a close relationship with us. Now it is time to take a look at our responsibility.

***Proverbs 18:24**, "A man that hath friends must shew himself friendly..."*

A great friendship is a two way street. Jesus has done His part, now it is time for you to show Him that you want to be one of His best friends. How do you do this? By showing yourself friendly.

Talk to Him. Walk with Him. Remember He is always with you. Seek His wisdom. Praise Him. Tell Him how much you need His wisdom and strength. Tell others about Him. Tell Him about others in your life. Speak honestly — that is what friends do! Thank Him for everything you enjoy. Christ desires to be your friend, but you need to return His friendship. You need to invest time and energy into your relationship with Christ.

6. We prove the sincerity of our friendship with Christ when we obey His commands.

John 15:14, *"Ye are my friends, if you do whatsoever I command you."*

If one of the teens in my church came to me and told me that he had a new friend, but then went on to explain that in order to prove his friendship to this person, he had to obey everything and anything this person told them to do — I'd be more than a little concerned! But in this regard, Jesus is different from any other friend. Jesus wants to be our friend, but we must always remember that He never stops being our God. He has every right to command us and to expect our obedience. No man can maintain a close relationship with God and live in rebellion toward His Word.

Proverbs 27:9, *"Ointment and perfume rejoice the heart: so doth the sweetness of a man's friend by hearty counsel."*

We need to view the Word of God for what it is – hearty counsel from a friend who loves us and has proven it by dying for us. Satan would like to turn your heart against the Bible by convincing you that its commands and principles rob you of fun and fulfillment. This of course is a lie!

Genesis 3:4-5, *"And the serpent said unto the woman, Ye shall not surely die: For God doth know that in the day ye eat thereof, then your eyes shall be opened, and ye shall be as gods, knowing good and evil."*

The world was plunged into sin because Adam and Eve listened to a lie. God is good. If He commands us to abstain from anything, we can be assured that it is for our own good. How can I show Jesus my friendship toward Him? I do so by choosing right over wrong.

7. ***The greatest obstacle preventing most Christians from developing a close friendship with God is worldliness.***

James 4:4, *"Ye adulterers and adulteresses, know ye not that the friendship of the world is enmity with God? whosoever therefore will be a friend of the world is the enemy of God."*

The biggest lie being told young people today is that you can be a friend of both the world and God. Worldliness has crept into the church: Young people who call themselves Christians sometimes dress immodestly, listen to the world's music, worship the world's heroes, and follow the world's entertainment and lifestyle. There is a cost to all of this. It is costing young people the ability to have a friendship with God.

Proverbs 27:17, *"Iron sharpeneth iron; so a man sharpeneth the countenance of his friend."*

Young people who separate themselves from worldliness, and draw near to God, find that their lives are sharpened – that they become prepared unto every good work. They begin to enjoy a spiritual prosperity and productivity the worldly Christian will never realize.

Check out your friends — your closest friends. Are they sharpening or dulling you? Get close to Jesus. Choose Him as your first and best friend. Then allow Him to help you choose your other friends.

Proverbs 13:20, *"He that walketh with wise men shall be wise: but a companion of fools shall be destroyed."*

What is Your Responsibility in This Relationship?

Remember, in every successful relationship, your concern needs to be focused on your responsibilities, not your perceived rights. Jesus has proven His love for us, and His desire to be our friend. Now the ball is in our court.

How badly do you want to be close to Jesus Christ? Is the Devil using something in your past to convince you that Jesus does not love you? Are you spurning the Savior because you would rather hear what you want to hear than what you need to hear? Are you investing in your relationship with Christ by taking the time to talk to Him and read His Word? Is disobedience and worldliness preventing you from being as close to Christ as you could be?

My advice to you: choose Christ! Choose Him over any other person or any other thing. Whatever is standing between you and the Savior, confess it, turn from it, and begin today the greatest of all relationships: a close friendship with your new best Friend.

Points to Ponder and Discuss:

1. What are some advantages of choosing Jesus as your best friend as opposed to an earthly friend?

2. What is the greatest proof of Christ's friendship toward us?

3. What is the greatest threat to the friendship we can enjoy with our Savior?

-4-

Your Relationship to God the Father

Lesson Goals:

1. To understand our responsibilities to God as outlined in the Bible.
2. To understand that the proper relationship results from fulfilling these responsibilities.
3. To evaluate ourselves in light of these truths.

Every relationship in life comes with responsibilities. These responsibilities are outlined in the Bible. A young person who does not have the proper relationship with God will find it difficult to have successful relationships with people. Your vertical relationship affects your horizontal relationships.

Every Christian teenager should both identify and seek to fulfill his responsibilities to God his Father.

A Teenager's Responsibilities to God

1. We are to love God.

Mark 12:28-30, *"And one of the scribes came, and having heard them reasoning together, and perceiving that he had answered them well, asked him, Which is the first commandment of all? And Jesus answered him, The first of all the commandments is, Hear, O Israel; The Lord our God is one Lord: And thou shalt love the Lord thy God with all thy heart, and with all thy soul, and with all thy mind, and with all thy strength: this is the first commandment."*

The first and greatest commandment that we have been given is to love the Lord our God. We are to love Him supremely, above everyone and everything. No person or thing should be loved more than God.

God is to have first place in our heart, in our soul, and in our mind. We are love him with all of our strength.

John 21:15-17, *"So when they had dined, Jesus saith to Simon Peter, Simon, son of Jonas, lovest thou me more than these? He saith unto him, Yea, Lord; thou knowest that I love thee. He saith unto him, Feed my lambs. He saith to him again the second time, Simon, son of Jonas, lovest thou me? He saith unto him, Yea, Lord; thou knowest that I love thee. He saith unto him, Feed my sheep. He saith unto him the third time, Simon, son of Jonas, lovest thou me? Peter was grieved because he said unto him the third time, Lovest thou me? And he said unto him, Lord, thou knowest all things; thou knowest that I love thee. Jesus saith unto him, Feed my sheep."*

The Apostle Peter went through a period of backsliding. He left the call of God upon his life and returned to his previous life. Jesus asked Peter three times, "Lovest thou me?" The first time Jesus added, "Lovest thou me more than these?" Jesus knew that Peter's problem was a love problem. Whenever we love anything more than we love the Son of God, that object becomes an idol unto us. No person or thing should ever hold a higher place in our hearts than God.

John Wesley once said, "Give me a hundred men who hate nothing but sin and love God with all their hearts and I will shake the world for Christ!"

Are you fulfilling your responsibility to God? Can you honestly say that you love the Lord first and foremost? Do you love Him with all of your heart, all of your mind, all of your soul, and all of your strength?

Above all — everyone and every thing — love God.

2. We are to fear God.

Psalm 33:8, *"Let all the earth fear the LORD: let all the inhabitants of the world stand in awe of him."*

Psalm 34:9, *"O fear the LORD, ye his saints: for there is no want to them that fear him."*

Proverbs 14:27, *"The fear of the LORD is a fountain of life, to depart from the snares of death."*

The second responsibility that we have in our relationship with God is to fear Him. Fear means to hold in reverence; to stand in awe of; to fear His chastening.

God is deserving of our respect and wonder. We should live our lives understanding that God blesses righteousness and punishes disobedience. He will not be mocked. God will not long tolerate a rebellious child.

Galatians 6:7-8, *"Be not deceived; God is not mocked: for whatsoever a man soweth, that shall he also reap. For he that soweth to his flesh shall of the flesh reap corruption; but he that soweth to the Spirit shall of the Spirit reap life everlasting."*

God's chastening is proof of His love for us. No good father would stand by and let one of his children head down a path that would lead to destruction without doing everything in his power to keep that child from doing so. God's chastisement in our lives is for our own good. Fear of God's chastisement is a wonderful motivation to keep us on the path of righteousness and blessing.

Hebrews 12:5-7, *"And ye have forgotten the exhortation which speaketh unto you as unto children, My son, despise not thou the chastening of the Lord, nor faint when thou art rebuked of him: For whom the Lord loveth he chasteneth, and scourgeth every son whom he receiveth. If ye endure chastening, God dealeth with you as with sons; for what son is he whom the father chasteneth not?"*

The fear of the Lord is the beginning of both knowledge and wisdom. Every teenager who loses his fear of God soon finds himself wandering down the road of foolishness. The fear of God keeps us out of Satan's minefields.

Proverbs 1:7, *"The fear of the LORD is the beginning of knowledge: but fools despise wisdom and instruction."*

Proverbs 9:10, *"The fear of the LORD is the beginning of wisdom: and the knowledge of the holy is understanding."*

Proverbs 14:27, *"The fear of the LORD is a fountain of life, to depart from the snares of death."*

Thomas à Kempis said, "Every man naturally desires knowledge; but what good is knowledge without fear of God? Indeed a humble rustic who serves God is better than a proud intellectual who neglects his soul to study the course of the stars."

3. We are to obey God.

Deuteronomy 11:26-28, *"Behold, I set before you this day a blessing and a curse; A blessing, if ye obey the commandments of the LORD your God, which I command you this day: And a curse, if ye will not obey the commandments of the LORD your God, but turn aside out of the way which I command you this day, to go after other gods, which ye have not known."*

A Christian has the responsibility to obey God. Without obedience, our relationship with the Lord will suffer. God promises blessings upon those who obey, and a curse upon those who refuse to obey. Obedience to God and His Word is foundational in our relationship to Him.

John 14:15, *"If ye love me, keep my commandments."*

John 15:10, *"If ye keep my commandments, ye shall abide in my love; even as I have kept my Father's commandments, and abide in his love."*

A. W. Tozer properly wrote, "Our Lord told His disciples that love and obedience were organically united. The final test of love is obedience."

Jesus tied our obedience to our love. We should obey God because we love God. It is one of the ways we can express to God our love for Him. Every time you obey what the Bible tells you to do, you tell God, "I love You." Every time you walk away from a temptation to do what God has told you NOT to do, you tell God, "I love You." Sadly, every time you disobey God your Father, you show Him that you love something or someone else more than you love Him.

The great revivalist, Charles Finney, once said, "A revival is nothing else than a new beginning of obedience to God."

4. We are to worship God.

Matthew 4:8-10, *"Again, the devil taketh him up into an exceeding high mountain, and sheweth him all the kingdoms of the world, and the glory of them; And saith unto him, All these things will I give thee, if thou wilt fall down and worship me. Then saith Jesus unto him, Get thee hence, Satan: for it is written, Thou shalt worship the Lord thy God, and him only shalt thou serve."*

Worship is reserved for God alone. You honor and obey your parents, but your worship is reserved for God. You respect your pastor, but you worship only God. You submit to God-placed authorities in your life, but you worship only God. Worship is for God and God alone.

Perhaps the greatest definition of worship I have read was written by R. A. Torrey. He wrote, "Worship is adoring contemplation of God."

According to Strong's Greek Bible Dictionary, the word "worship" means "to kiss, like a dog licking his master's hand; to crouch or fawn; literally to prostrate oneself in homage and reverence; to adore."

Psalm 95:6, *"O come, let us worship and bow down: let us kneel before the LORD our maker."*

Our worship is reflected in our willingness to bow before God. When God sees a Christian bow his knee, or prostrate himself on the ground, He accepts that as worship. God, of course, also looks upon the heart of a man! A man can physically bow his knee, but his heart remain proud and unyielding. When we bow our knee, we should also humble our heart. From this position of humility, we then can offer to God the reverence and adoration He so completely deserves.

Here is a fair question: have you ever truly worshipped God?

John 4:24, *"God is a Spirit: and they that worship him must worship him in spirit and in truth."*

Philippians 3:3, *"For we are the circumcision, which worship God in the spirit, and rejoice in Christ Jesus, and have no confidence in the flesh."*

Worship is an act of the spirit of a man. True worship does not flow from our flesh or from our soul. It must be generated from our reborn spirit. Because of this, only a saved, born-again Christian can worship God. Reverence, adoration, praise, and love should flow to God above from the reborn spirit of every Christian on earth. Spiritual worship may affect us physically, and it may affect our mind, heart, and will, but it is always generated from our spirit.

Much of what is labeled as "praise and worship" in the modern-day, contemporary churches is nothing more than an attempt to excite the flesh and arouse the emotions of people. Worship in the Bible is almost always private, not public, and is always an act of the spirit, not the flesh. Learn to worship God privately and spiritually. Do not get caught up in today's fake and fleshly worship services.

Psalm 29:2, *"Give unto the LORD the glory due unto his name; worship the LORD in the beauty of holiness."*

True worship flows from a holy life, and produces holiness within us. Again, much of the "flesh fests" of today's false churches mock the very holiness of God! It is centered on what WE get out of it, not what GOD gets out of it. It is often led by those whose lives are baptized in worldliness, immodesty, and hypocrisy. You cannot separate worship and holiness. In order to worship God, we must come with clean hands and a pure heart.

Psalm 95:6, *"O come, let us worship and bow down: let us kneel before the LORD our maker."*

Psalm 96:9, *"O worship the LORD in the beauty of holiness: fear before him, all the earth."*

Psalm 99:9, *"Exalt the LORD our God, and worship at his holy hill; for the LORD our God is holy."*

5. We are to glorify God.

1 Corinthians 10:31, *"Whether therefore ye eat, or drink, or whatsoever ye do, do all to the glory of God."*

What an amazing and all-inclusive verse! "Whatsoever ye do!" Our words, our actions, our attitudes, our decisions – ALL are to bring glory to God. MUCH of what we do – if we were to be honest – is done in an attempt to bring glory to ourselves. Let me say it again – much of what we do is done in an attempt to bring glory to ourselves! The wise and mature young person weighs his words and actions carefully, saying and doing only those things that will bring God glory.

1 Corinthians 3:21, *"Therefore let no man glory in men."*

2 Corinthians 10:17, *"But he that glorieth, let him glory in the Lord."*

1 Timothy 1:17, *"Now unto the King eternal, immortal, invisible, the only wise God, be honour and glory for ever and ever. Amen."*

David Brainerd wrote, "We should always look upon ourselves as God's servants, placed in God's world, to do His work… not with a design to grow rich and great, but to glorify God, and do all the good we possibly can."

6. We are to serve God.

John 12:26, *"If any man serve me, let him follow me; and where I am, there shall also my servant be: if any man serve me, him will my Father honour."*

1 Thessalonians 1:9, *"For they themselves shew of us what manner of entering in we had unto you, and how ye turned to God from idols to serve the living and true God;"*

It is an honor and a privilege to serve the Lord! God is to be served by His people. He is our Master, we are His servants. What He wants is more important than what we want. His work is to take precedence over our work. His will is to be honored above our will.

Psalm 100:2, *"Serve the LORD with gladness..."*

As we serve the Lord, we are to do it with gladness. Serving God is not something we HAVE to do, but it should be viewed as something we GET to do! What an honor to serve the King of Kings and Lord of Lords!

Charles Spurgeon wrote, "If we give God service it must be because He gives us grace. We work for Him because He works in us."

As a seventeen year-old young man, I committed my life to serve the Lord. Outside of salvation, it was the greatest decision of my life. Take every opportunity you are presented to serve the Lord. There is no greater life.

7. We are to trust God.

Psalm 18:2, *"The LORD is my rock, and my fortress, and my deliverer; my God, my strength, in whom I will trust; my buckler, and the horn of my salvation, and my high tower."*

Psalm 37:5, *"Commit thy way unto the LORD; trust also in him; and he shall bring it to pass."*

Proverbs 3:5-6, *"Trust in the LORD with all thine heart; and lean not unto thine own understanding. In all thy ways acknowledge him, and he shall direct thy paths."*

God is good. He can be trusted. His ways are perfect. In our relationship to God, we have the responsibility to trust Him.

Trust is not required when we understand what God is doing. Trust is required when we DO NOT understand what He is doing in our lives. God asks for our trust. He is honored when we learn to trust Him.

The Bible urges you to trust in the Lord "with all thine heart." Make the decision early in your life that no matter what happens, no matter how it may seem from a human perspective, you will put your trust in the Lord.

Charles Spurgeon wrote, "We cannot always trace God's hand, but we can always trust God's heart."

God understands that it takes both blessings and trials to form us into what He needs us to be. God will sometimes allow difficult things to come into our lives! We need the valleys as well as the mountaintops. No matter what happens, no matter what you have to face in life, TRUST GOD!!! He is your Father, and He cares for you!

Every relationship comes with responsibilities. Our relationship to God is no exception. We have the responsibility to love Him, fear Him and obey Him. We are commanded to worship Him and to make sure that everything we do brings Him glory. We also are to serve him with gladness and to trust Him no matter what the circumstances of life may be. The man who fulfills these responsibilities becomes a delight to his Heavenly Father and can be assured of God's blessings and presence in his life.

Points to Ponder and Discuss:

1. How can we both love God and fear Him?

2. What does it mean to worship the Lord, "in spirit and in truth"?

3. Why is it impossible to both trust the Lord and also understand everything that He allows?

-5-

Your Relationship to the Holy Spirit (Part 1)

Lesson Goals:

1. To understand the Holy Spirit's part in our salvation.
2 To understand all that a proper relationship with the Holy Spirit offers each believer.

God is one God. Yet He chooses to reveal Himself to us in three distinct personalities — God the Father, God the Son and God the Holy Spirit. Our relationship to each member of the Godhead is important. Yet many Christians miss out on having a real and personal relationship with the Holy Spirit of God. Some have never uttered a word to Him, never acknowledged His presence in their lives, and have never accessed all that He wishes to do for them and through them.

Let me introduce to you the member of the Divine Trinity who — if you are saved — dwells inside of you this very moment. My hope is that today you will start a close and sweet relationship with the Spirit of God.

A. W. Tozer wrote, "The Spirit-filled life is not a special, deluxe edition of Christianity. It is part and parcel of the total plan of God for His people."

The Holy Spirit's Involvement in Our New Birth

John 3:3-8, *"Jesus answered and said unto him, Verily, verily, I say unto thee, Except a man be born* *again, he cannot see the kingdom of God. Nicodemus saith unto him, How can a man be born when he is old? can he enter the second time into his mother's womb, and be born? Jesus answered, Verily, verily, I say unto thee, Except a man be born of water and of the Spirit, he cannot enter into the kingdom of God. That which is born of the flesh is flesh; and that which is born of the Spirit is spirit. Marvel not that I said unto thee, Ye must be born again. The wind bloweth where it listeth, and thou hearest the sound thereof, but canst not tell whence it cometh, and whither it goeth: so is every one that is born of the Spirit."*

Genesis 2:17, *"But of the tree of the knowledge of good and evil, thou shalt not eat of it: for in the day that thou eatest thereof thou shalt surely die."*

Notice the phrase, "in the day that thou eatest." The very day that they ate the forbidden fruit, they died. We can read the story and know that they did not die physically on that day. Their souls did not die, for the soul of man never dies — it will live somewhere forever. What part of man died that day? The spirit of man died.

Jesus told Nicodemus, "Except a man be born again, he cannot see the kingdom of God." We are born physically alive, with a never-dying soul, but we are also born spiritually dead — literally with a dead spirit. Salvation occurs when we believe the Gospel of Jesus Christ, and make the decision to receive Him as our personal Savior. At that moment, the Spirit of God comes within us and regenerates our dead spirit. The Holy Spirit brings to life that part of us that sin killed.

1 Peter 3:18, *"For Christ also hath once suffered for sins, the just for the unjust, that he might bring us to God, being put to death in the flesh, but quickened by the Spirit:"*

Our Body Becomes the Temple of the Holy Spirit

Once the Holy Spirit comes into our bodies to perform the miracle of the new birth, He never leaves. The

Holy Spirit literally takes up residence inside of every newborn Christian, and our bodies become His dwelling place.

1 Corinthians 3:16, *"Know ye not that ye are the temple of God, and that the Spirit of God dwelleth in you?"*

1 Corinthians 6:19-20, *"What? know ye not that your body is the temple of the Holy Ghost which is in you, which ye have of God, and ye are not your own? For ye are bought with a price: therefore glorify God in your body, and in your spirit, which are God's."*

Stop and let that sink in. If you are saved, a member of the divine Trinity, God the Holy Spirit, lives inside of you! The Holy Spirit is a person, Someone you can communicate with, talk to, listen to, walk with — Someone with whom you can have a sweet and special relationship.

In 1994, my wife and I purchased a fixer-upper house north of Jasonville, Indiana. Even though it needed a lot of work, we immediately moved in. From that day to this, we have transformed that original structure. Year by year, project by project, we have remodeled each and every room in this house. We also have added on to this house, enlarging its borders and making it more pleasant, more functional, and more to our liking. It is still not perfect, but it is amazing the transformation that has taken place from the day we moved in till now.

This is exactly what the Holy Spirit wants to do in your life. God purchased you with the blood of His own Son, Jesus Christ. The Holy Spirit took possession of your body the day you were saved. His job is to take this "fixer-upper" project and transform it into the image of Jesus Christ — to make it more pleasant, more functional, and more to God's liking.

Augustine wrote, "Breathe in me, O Holy Spirit, that my thoughts may all be holy. Act in me, O Holy Spirit, that my work, too, may be holy. Draw my heart, O Holy Spirit, that I love but what is holy. Strengthen me, O Holy Spirit, to defend all that is holy. Guard me, then, O Holy Spirit, that I always may be holy."

The Ministry of the Holy Spirit

What does the Holy Spirit want to accomplish in our lives? What are the benefits of having His presence? Why should we strive to build and maintain a close relationship to this often forgotten Guest?

1. The Spirit comforts us in our affliction.

John 14:16-17, *"And I will pray the Father, and he shall give you another Comforter, that he may abide with you for ever; Even the Spirit of truth; whom the world cannot receive, because it seeth him not, neither knoweth him: but ye know him; for he dwelleth with you, and shall be in you."*

Acts 9:31, *"Then had the churches rest throughout all Judaea and Galilee and Samaria, and were edified; and walking in the fear of the Lord, and in the comfort of the Holy Ghost, were multiplied."*

I have been in the ministry for over thirty years. As a pastor, you find yourself thrust into the best and the worst days of people's lives. Heartache, disappointment, sickness and death — these are all the results of sin, and as long as we live on this sin-cursed planet, these things will come into every person's life.

Christians who have a close relationship with the Holy Spirit of God benefit from the comfort that He brings to them during these dark valley experiences. I have watched the Comforter literally carry people through the crucibles of life. I have seen Him turn their sorrow to smiles and their heartaches to hope. I have also, sadly, watched those without His presence self-destruct during times of tribulation. The Holy Spirit wants to be your Comforter.

2. The Spirit tutors us in God's Word.

1 Corinthians 2:11-13, *"For what man knoweth the things of a man, save the spirit of man which is in him? even so the things of God knoweth no man, but the Spirit of God. Now we have received, not the spirit of the world, but the spirit which is of God; that we might know the things that are freely given to us of God. Which things also we speak, not in the words which man's wisdom teacheth, but which the Holy Ghost teacheth; comparing spiritual things with spiritual."*

Have you ever read the Bible and had a difficult time understanding it? We have all been there. One of the jobs of the Holy Spirit is to open up our understanding as we study the Word of God. This is one of the great benefits of having a close relationship to the Holy Spirit.

I have written several books. Years ago, I received a telephone call from a teenage young man. He wanted to ask me to explain a paragraph that he was reading in my book, *The Teenage Years of Jesus Christ*. I was so pleased that he called, and took joy in bringing light to that particular section of the book. As he hung up he said to me, "Thank you for taking my call. It sure helped to talk to the author of the book. After all, who better to explain what it means?"

The Holy Spirit was used of God to deliver the very words of God. Who better to explain what they mean?

2 Peter 1:20-21, *"Knowing this first, that no prophecy of the scripture is of any private interpretation. For the prophecy came not in old time by the will of man: but holy men of God spake as they were moved by the Holy Ghost."*

3. The Spirit partners with us in prayer.

Romans 8:26-27, *"Likewise the Spirit also helpeth our infirmities: for we know not what we should pray for as we ought: but the Spirit itself maketh intercession for us with groanings which cannot be uttered. And he that searcheth the hearts knoweth what is the mind of the Spirit, because he maketh intercession for the saints according to the will of God."*

Have you ever prayed together with someone? In many churches, members are assigned prayer partners — someone with whom they could meet on a regular basis for a time of prayer. It is a particular joy for me to pray with other men of my church. But the best prayer partner any of us can have is the One who lives inside of us — the sweet Holy Spirit of God.

The Holy Spirit wants to help us pray. He wants to guide us as we choose for what and for whom to pray. The Bible teaches us that He also prays for us when we sometimes do not know exactly what to pray.

Young person, many times in life you will be faced with a decision where there is no clear right or wrong choice. It may be which job to pursue or which college to attend. Sometimes we don't know how to pray. During these times, it is wonderful to have the Spirit of God make "intercession for us." When you don't know how to pray, ask the Holy Spirit to pray for you, and to lead you into His perfect will for your life.

Ephesians 6:18, *"Praying always with all prayer and supplication in the Spirit, and watching thereunto with all perseverance and supplication for all saints;"*

As a pastor, I am asked from time to time to give advice. People tend to come and meet with their pastor when the decisions are pretty important. Many times I cannot tell them which path to take, but I can pray with them — supplicate for them in the Spirit. I can ask the Holy Spirit to reveal to them the perfect will of God.

What a blessing that we share the same Holy Spirit! And if we are tender to His leading, we will be guided well.

4. The Spirit gives us the assurance of our salvation.

Romans 8:16, *"The Spirit itself beareth witness with our spirit, that we are the children of God:"*

I have met many teenagers who struggle with the assurance of their salvation. Sometimes a young person's doubt is because they have never been saved. But more often, a young person begins to doubt their salvation as a result of having a strained relationship with the Holy Spirit of God. The voice of the Holy Spirit will provide assurance that we are the children of God. If you begin to grieve or quench His working in your life, then that voice of assurance is also quieted.

A young person who has a proper and close relationship with the Holy Spirit seldom battles with doubts concerning their salvation.

5. The Spirit directs us to divine appointments.

Acts 8:29-31, *"Then the Spirit said unto Philip, Go near, and join thyself to this chariot. And Philip ran thither to him, and heard him read the prophet Esaias, and said, Understandest thou what thou readest? And he said, How can I, except some man should guide me? And he desired Philip that he would come up and sit with him."*

We see the work of the Holy Spirit in both of these men. The lost man sits in the chariot seeking the truth of God's Word. A saved man is specifically directed to him to help him discover the truth of the Gospel. Both men are being dealt with by the Spirit of God.

Early in my ministry training, God taught me the importance of listening to the leading of His Spirit. I visited in inner city Chicago most weekends during my Bible college years. I had visited the same general neighborhood for several months, witnessing for Christ and inviting people to church. On this particular day, the Spirit of God kept bringing to mind a family who used to attend our church, but had moved out of the neighborhood. It had been weeks since that move, but I could not get them out of my mind. I felt compelled to go and visit the third floor apartment where they had lived. My rational mind kept arguing against the notion, because it had been weeks since they had lived there.

Finally, I gave in to God's leading and climbed the stairs to this apartment. I knocked, and, as I suspected, it was vacant. I climbed down to the second floor and felt compelled to try that door, but again, no one was home. By now I fely really foolish, but when I came to the bottom floor apartment, again there was this intense leading to knock on the door. It looked vacant — no curtains, no furniture in the living room, no light that I could see. But I knocked anyway. To my surprise, I heard footsteps, then the door swung open and a twenty-something young man stood staring at me.

"You came!" he said as he grabbed my hand and dragged me in. He took me to the back room where there was a mattress on the floor, a small table, two chairs, and a dim lamp. On the table were two things — an open Bible and a .38 revolver. Needless to say, I was a bit nervous at this point!

He told me his name was Frank. His wife had left him a week or so before, and he had hit rock bottom. He told me that he had been reading the Bible, but could not find the answers he needed. Frank then shared with me something I will never forget.

"I told God that I was going to sit down here, read the Bible, and wait for Him to send someone to help me find what I am looking for. If that someone didn't come by midnight, I was going to shoot myself."

I sat at that table and led Frank to Christ. He came to church the next day, and was baptized. I was able to help Frank get in touch with his wife, and God performed a miracle in giving that marriage a second chance.

I learned something that day — listen to the voice of the Spirit of God! And keep a good relationship with Him so that nothing hinders His voice.

6. The Spirit Convicts Us When We Do Wrong

1 Thessalonians 4:7-8, *"For God hath not called us unto uncleanness, but unto holiness. He therefore that despiseth, despiseth not man, but God, who hath also given unto us his holy Spirit."*

John 16:7-8, *"Nevertheless I tell you the truth; It is expedient for you that I go away: for if I go not away, the Comforter will not come unto you; but if I depart, I will send him unto you. And when he is come, he will reprove the world of sin, and of righteousness, and of judgment:"*

Most Christians are pleased to have the Holy Spirit's comfort. They also appreciate the assurance He gives as well as His help in prayer, understanding the Bible, and divine direction. But too many times all of this is hindered by how we respond to the conviction of the Holy Spirit. In the next chapter, we will study how we damage this important relationship, and if we have done so, how to repair this damage.

Billy Sunday reminded Christians in his preaching, "A revival does two things. First, it returns the Church from her backsliding and second, it causes the conversion of men and women; and it always includes the conviction of sin on the part of the Church."

We need this work of the Holy Spirit to keep our hearts right and clean. How is your relationship with the

Holy Spirit? Do you hear His still, small voice? Are you willing to listen and follow His leading?

Points to Ponder and Discuss:

1. What does it mean to you for your body to be the temple of the Holy Spirit?

2. How important is it to involve the Holy Spirit in our daily Bible reading and prayer time?

3. Have you ever experienced a divine appointment?

-6-

Your Relationship to the Holy Spirit (Part 2)

Lesson Goals:

1. To understand how we can damage our relationship to the Holy Spirit.
2. To learn how to repair this important relationship.

The Holy Spirit's Arch Nemesis

Galatians 5:16-17, *"This I say then, Walk in the Spirit, and ye shall not fulfil the lust of the flesh. For the flesh lusteth against the Spirit, and the Spirit against the flesh: and these are contrary the one to the other: so that ye cannot do the things that ye would."*

Sadly, there is a part of us that works against what the Holy Spirit is trying to do in our lives. Although we are born again, and although we now have a reborn spirit AND the indwelling of the Holy Spirit, our flesh still stubbornly wars against the changes that need to be made in our lives. The greatest obstacle that stands between us and Christlikeness is not the Devil, and not the world, but our own flesh. The appetites of our flesh war against the appetites of our newborn spirit. This battle rages inside of every Christian. Thankfully, we have the Holy Spirit of God living inside of us to assist us in this battle. The more we give ourselves over to His control, the less problem we have with our flesh. But the more we ignore, grieve or quench His working in our lives, the harder it is to live a victorious Christian life.

Thomas Watson penned this stern warning: "The pampering of the flesh is the quenching of God's Spirit."

Our Responsibilities to the Holy Spirit

Remember, the secret to successful relationships is found in one word — responsibility. We saw in the last chapter that there are many wonderful benefits that we enjoy as a result of being indwelt by the Spirit of God, but what about our part? What responsibilities do we carry in this relationship?

1. We are to be led by the Holy Spirit.

Romans 8:1, *"There is therefore now no condemnation to them which are in Christ Jesus, who walk not after the flesh, but after the Spirit."*

It is vitally important for us to learn to be yielded to the leading of the Holy Spirit. As we go about our duties each day, we need to develop a Holy Spirit sensitivity — an inner ear if you will. This allows us to hear His voice, and to sense His direction in our lives.

The average driver has become increasingly dependent upon the GPS (Global Positioning System) available on most smart phones. We type in where we want to go, and the GPS will give us step by step directions. Many put total faith in this technology, sometimes at risk of their very lives! Here are some true stories of where some have ended up by listening to their GPS:

One man was stopped by police as he was driving down a railroad track. He told them his GPS told him to take a right at the railroad crossing.

Or the three girls visiting the United States from France. They landed at the airport, rented a Mercedes SUV, typed in their destination in the GPS device, and found themselves 20 minutes later in a lake. The driver told police, "My GPS told me to make a right into the lake."

Or the Japanese tourist who drove into the Pacific Ocean because his GPS directed him to do so.

Or the American truck driver who spent 10 days in jail after his GPS directed him to drive his chemical tanker into the side of an elementary school building. Again, he told the police, "I was just following instructions."

Then there were the six friends in England who decided to spend a day holiday shopping in France. Their GPS took them instead to Belgium. They missed France by 96 miles.

My favorite? The Australian limo driver who followed his GPS down a flight of stairs outside of a crowded mall. He, his limo, and his boss were treated to a rather bumpy ride down 68 cement stairs. He was fired from his job, but don't worry — he has since found a new career in air traffic control!

When we get saved, God gives us His Spirit! How sad that we are willing to put total faith in what has proven to be imperfect technology, but fail to listen and follow the leading of the Holy Spirit of God in our lives.

Galatians 5:16, *"This I say then, Walk in the Spirit, and ye shall not fulfil the lust of the flesh."*

2. We are to seek the filling of the Spirit.

What does the Bible mean when it commands us to be filled with the Spirit? Remember, the Holy Spirit is a person, not a gas or a liquid. You either have Him or you don't. Being filled with the Spirit of God is not you getting more of Him, but Him getting more of you.

Acts 4:31, *"And when they had prayed, the place was shaken where they were assembled together; and they* *were all filled with the Holy Ghost, and they spake the word of God with boldness."*

Acts 13:52, *"And the disciples were filled with joy, and with the Holy Ghost."*

Ephesians 5:18, *"And be not drunk with wine, wherein is excess; but be filled with the Spirit;"*

In order to be filled, we must first be emptied. Two things fill our lives and prevent the Spirit of God from having control — our sin and ourselves.

In order to be filled, we must first get clean. Confessing and forsaking our sins prepares our hearts to be filled and controlled by the Holy Spirit.

Then we have to get self out of the way. Who is sitting in the driver's seat of your life? As long as you insist on stubbornly holding on to the steering wheel and directing your own life, the Holy Spirit will let you continue to drive yourself into one mess after another. Let the Spirit of God lead the way.

Corrie Ten Boom wrote, "Trying to do the Lord's work in your own strength is the most confusing, exhausting, and tedious of all work. But when you are filled with the Holy Spirit, then the ministry of Jesus just flows out of you."

3. We are commanded not to grieve the Holy Spirit.

Ephesians 4:29-32, *"Let no corrupt communication proceed out of your mouth, but that which is good to the use of edifying, that it may minister grace unto the hearers. And grieve not the holy Spirit of God, whereby ye are sealed unto the day of redemption. Let all bitterness, and wrath, and anger, and clamour, and evil speaking, be put away from you, with all malice: And be ye kind one to another, tenderhearted, forgiving one another, even as God for Christ's sake hath forgiven you."*

The sins dealt with in this portion of Scripture can grieve the Holy Spirit inside of us. The word "grieve" means "to distress, to sadden, to cause one to be heavy with sorrow." Corrupt communications grieve the Spirit of God. Our words can hurt not only others and our testimony — they can also hurt the Holy Spirit.

Bitterness, wrath, anger, clamour, evil speaking, malice, unkindness, hard-heartedness, an unforgiving spirit — all of these cause the Spirit of God great sorrow in our lives. They break His heart. They also damage our relationship with Him.

Charles Spurgeon wrote, "This day, my God, I hate sin… because it has done Thee wrong. To have grieved my God is the worst grief to me."

Would to God we would all feel the same.

4. We are warned against quenching the Holy Spirit.

1 Thessalonians 5:19, *"Quench not the Spirit."*

Although the Holy Spirit will never leave the believer, we can get to the point where He no longer attempts to communicate with us. If we will not heed His still, small voice then God will bring other things into our lives to get our attention.

Be careful that you do not harden your heart against the Spirit of God. To quench His working in your life is a serious matter. Here is a fair question: when was the last time you clearly heard the voice of God's Spirit in your life? Can you point to a time when you were personally comforted by Him? Taught, directed, or convicted by Him? Has His voice grown quiet in your life? Could it be that you have quenched the Spirit's activity in your life because of your refusal to be corrected by Him?

2 Chronicles 30:8, *"Now be ye not stiffnecked, as your fathers were, but yield yourselves unto the LORD,* *and enter into his sanctuary, which he hath sanctified for ever: and serve the LORD your God, that the fierceness of his wrath may turn away from you."*

5. We should beware of tempting the Holy Spirit.

Acts 5:9-10, *"Then Peter said unto her, How is it that ye have agreed together to tempt the Spirit of the Lord? behold, the feet of them which have buried thy husband are at the door, and shall carry thee out. Then fell she down straightway at his feet, and yielded up the ghost: and the young men came in, and found her dead, and, carrying her forth, buried her by her husband."*

Ananias and Sapphira conspired in their hearts to lie to the apostles. They sold a piece of property and publicly claimed to have given the money to the Lord's work while privately holding back some of it for their own use. What they failed to understand is that they were not lying to men, they were lying to the Holy Spirit. This sin cost them their lives.

It is a dangerous thing to refuse to confront and fix a damaged relationship with the Spirit of God. Take a minute and examine your life. Are you daily committing sins that are causing the Holy Spirit grief and shame? Have you gotten to the point where you have completely quenched His working in your life? Could it be that you are lying to the Holy Ghost — or about Him? Are you using Him as an excuse to do what you want to do while claiming His direction and approval? Could it be that you are one sin away from God saying, "Enough!"?

Repairing Your Relationship with the Holy Spirit

I heard a preacher say this as he was conducting the invitation at the conclusion of his sermon: "There are probably two reasons why you should come to the altar and do business with the Lord. You should come if you feel the Holy Spirit telling you to come. And just as importantly, you should come if you haven't heard from the Holy Spirit in a very long time."

I do not believe that he was manipulating the audience to get more people to the altar. I believe he spoke the truth. I have had born-again Christians tell me that it has been years since they have felt the working of the Spirit of God in their hearts. I cannot lay the fault of this lack of communication at the feet of God's Holy Spirit. If we are not hearing from Him regularly, it is because of the hardness of our hearts. We very well may have quenched His working in our lives. If so, how do we get back to where we once were? How is that sweet relationship restored?

1.) You do NOT need to get saved again. Biblically speaking, it is impossible to be saved "again." Right now, you are either saved or lost. If you are saved, going through the motions of getting "saved again" will not fix the real problem. The lack of assurance you have about your salvation is probably not because you are not saved, but because you have quenched the voice of the One who provides that assurance.

2.) You do need to spend some time in soul searching. Think back. Was there a time when the voice of the Holy Spirit was strong in your life? What happened to change that relationship? What sin has gotten in the way? Who is it in your life that you are more interested in pleasing rather than the Spirit of God?

3) You do need to ask the Holy Spirit to forgive you and to restore your broken relationship. God's capacity to forgive is beyond our human comprehension. Be assured, God loves you. Jesus loves you. And yes, the Holy Spirit loves you. Be willing to ask for His forgiveness. Start reaching out to Him and rebuilding that relationship.

4) Make a vow to stay tender to the voice of the Holy Spirit from this point forward.

It is a wonderful privilege for us to have fellowship with God. A right relationship with the Holy Spirit of God is the key to keeping our fellowship sweet.

I'll finish this chapter with a quote from Andrew Murray. "Men ought to seek with their whole hearts to be filled with the Spirit of God. Without being filled with the Spirit, it is utterly impossible that an individual Christian or a church can ever live or work as God desires."

Points to Ponder and Discuss:

1. What does it mean to be filled with the Holy Spirit?
2. Which sins are specifically listed as those that can grieve the Holy Spirit?
3. What does it mean to quench the Holy Spirit?

-7-

Your Relationship to Your Parents

Lesson Goals:

1. To discover our responsibilities to our parents.
2. To evaluate how successful we are in performing these responsibilities.
3. To be reminded of the blessings and the consequences attached to these responsibilities.

Who Are Your Parents?

When you enter your teenage years, it is a good time to step back and really look at your mom and dad. It is time to start seeing them a bit differently. Your mom was once a little girl. She was once a teenager. Have you ever taken the time to get to know her — not just as your mom, but as a person?

Your dad was once a young boy. In what kind of home was he raised? What were the dynamics of his family life? What personal disappointments or tragedies shaped his life? It is time to get to know your dad so that you can better understand your dad.

As a teenager, it is easy to begin to notice inconsistencies in your parents — to put them under a microscope of criticism. Your mom and dad are not perfect, but they are perfect for you. I know this because God chose them for you, and God does not make mistakes.

Whether they are Christians or non-believers, God has given you responsibilities for your relationship with your parents. What are these Biblical responsibilities?

A Teenager's Responsibilities to His Parents

1. You are to honor your parents.

Exodus 20:12, *"Honour thy father and thy mother: that thy days may be long upon the land which the LORD thy God giveth thee."*

Ephesians 6:2-3, *"Honour thy father and mother; (which is the first commandment with promise;) That it may be well with thee, and thou mayest live long on the earth."*

The word "honour" means "to prize, to affix a proper valuation upon, to revere." Let's be honest — most of us undervalue our parents. It is so easy to take for granted the things they do for us every day of our lives. Parenting may seem easy, but it is not. Your parents work, love, invest and sacrifice for you. In return, the Bible says that you are to properly honor them.

In both the Old and New Testaments, this command to honor your parents comes with a promised reward! Honoring your parents will secure for you God's promise of a good life (that it may be well with thee), and an extended life (...and that thou mayest live long on the earth).

How do you honor your parents? You honor your parents by making them feel valuable to you.

1) Parents feel valued when you want to spend time with them. During your teen years, it is very easy to become more interested in spending time with your friends than with your parents. Although enjoying and investing in good friendships can certainly be a blessing, you need to plan some time each week to spend with Mom and Dad. Share in their interests and hobbies. Ask to help with a project they are working on. Let them know that you enjoy spending time with them.

2) Parents feel valued when you seek their opinions and their advice. Your parents have a lifetime of knowledge and wisdom that they would like to share with you. When you dismiss their opinions and ignore their advice, you dishonor your mom and dad.

3) Parents feel valued when you express appreciation for their work and their sacrifice. Next time Mom fixes a meal for you, give her a peck on the cheek and say, "Thanks, Mom." Next time your dad goes out of his way to do something nice for you, give him a hug and a "thank you." You will be shocked what this does for them.

2. You are to obey your parents.

Romans 1:28-30, *"And even as they did not like to retain God in their knowledge, God gave them over to a reprobate mind, to do those things which are not convenient; Being filled with all unrighteousness, fornication, wickedness, covetousness, maliciousness; full of envy, murder, debate, deceit, malignity; whisperers, Backbiters, haters of God, despiteful, proud, boasters, inventors of evil things, disobedient to parents..."*

Colossians 3:20, *"Children, obey your parents in all things: for this is well pleasing unto the Lord."*

2 Timothy 3:1-2, *"This know also, that in the last days perilous times shall come. For men shall be lovers of their own selves, covetous, boasters, proud, blasphemers, disobedient to parents, unthankful, unholy..."*

Proverbs 30:17, *"The eye that mocketh at his father, and despiseth to obey his mother, the ravens of the valley shall pick it out, and the young eagles shall eat it."*

Some teenagers decide that because they are becoming a young man or a young woman, they no longer have to obey their parents. God does not agree with this rebellious and worldly opinion. One day, young man, God will bring you a young lady for you to love and to marry. At that time, you will "leave and cleave." You will begin a new home and a new family. You will no longer be living in your parents' home or be under their direct authority. But, until then, you are to be obedient to your parents.

Young man, do you want to live a full life? Do you want God's blessing upon your life? Young lady, do you want it to be well with you? Do you want to live long upon this earth? Stop mimicking the rebellion of this pagan culture and obey the Bible. Love your parents and gift them your obedient heart.

3. You are to learn from your parents.

Proverbs 1:8, *"My son, hear the instruction of thy father, and forsake not the law of thy mother:"*

Proverbs 4:1, *"Hear, ye children, the instruction of a father, and attend to know understanding.*

Young person, your parents have so much to teach you! But you have to participate in the process — you have to be willing to learn.

The Bible teaches us in the above verses that learning starts with hearing. Listening is a discipline that is almost lost in this generation. The Devil has plugged young people into technology and has at the same time, unplugged them from their families. Take out your ear buds and learn to listen to your parents. Turn off your cell phones and video games and engage your parents in conversation. Listen to them.

Your mom and dad have a lifetime of experiences and lessons to pass on to you. Once they pass away, it is too late. What they know will have died with them, and you will be the poorer for it if you failed to receive what they were trying to hand down to you.

The most skilled and gifted young men in our church are the young men who took the time to learn from their dads and grandfathers. The best prepared and most successful young wives and mothers in our church are those who took the time to listen and to learn from their mothers and grandmothers.

Let me ask you this — what is your dad really good at? What is your mother's expertise? Have you let them teach you? You might say, "Well, they never offered?" So? Have you ever asked?

Learning what they know not only helps you to obtain the knowledge they possess, but it also benefits both of you because of the time you spend together in the process. These times will produce future memories and those, my young friend, will someday be priceless.

The year my dad turned 70, I approached him with a project. I handed him a list of fourteen different people groups — children, teenagers, moms, dads, grandparents, church members, pastors, soul winners, etc. Based on his 70 years of life, and 40 years of ministry experience, I asked him to write out 5 pieces of advice that he would give to each of these people groups. It took him several months, but he at last handed me the finished product. I had no idea that within a year of him completing that project, he would be in Heaven. I cannot tell you how valuable that written advice has been to me and my family.

4. You are to show respect to your parents.

Exodus 21:17, *"And he that curseth his father, or his mother, shall surely be put to death."*

Leviticus 19:3, *"Ye shall fear every man his mother, and his father, and keep my sabbaths: I am the LORD your God."*

Deuteronomy 27:16, *"Cursed be he that setteth light by his father or his mother. And all the people shall say, Amen."*

It is almost unthinkable the way many teenagers treat their parents. The lack of respect has reached the level of wickedness. God hears it, God warns against it, and God promises to revenge it.

Thankfully, most Christian young people respect their parents. You have a chance to show your generation a better way. There are many ways to show respect to your parents.

1) Show respect in the way you address your parents. Never be disrespectful in either your words or the tone of your voice. You should never raise your voice in anger to your parents. Be kind to them, and think of ways to compliment them. Express often your appreciation.

2) Show respect in the way you talk to others about your parents. Always hold them in high esteem. Do not criticize your parents. If you have something that is bothering you, you should go and talk to them about it. If you do so respectfully, they will likely receive it and consider your point of view.

3) Show respect in the way you treat your parents. As a teenager, you now have the strength and maturity to step in and make life easier for Mom and Dad. Volunteer to take over some of the household chores and duties. Young men, hold open the door for your mother. Be considerate of her wishes and tender to her fears. In every way possible, honor the wishes of both your parents and do everything you can to make them happy.

It is a sin to be disrespectful to your mother or father. If that sin has crept into your life, confess it to God, and make it right with your parents. By doing so, you stave off God's judgment and secure God's blessings.

5. We are to care for our parents.

John 19:25-27, *"Now there stood by the cross of Jesus his mother, and his mother's sister, Mary the wife of*

Cleophas, and Mary Magdalene. When Jesus therefore saw his mother, and the disciple standing by, whom he loved, he saith unto his mother, Woman, behold thy son! Then saith he to the disciple, Behold thy mother! And from that hour that disciple took her unto his own home."

1 Timothy 5:3-8, *"Honour widows that are widows indeed. But if any widow have children or nephews, let them learn first to shew piety at home, and to requite their parents: for that is good and acceptable before God... But if any provide not for his own, and specially for those of his own house, he hath denied the faith, and is worse than an infidel."*

Proverbs 23:22, *"Hearken unto thy father that begat thee, and despise not thy mother when she is old."*

My dad was always the strongest man I knew. As a boy, I would try and help him as best as I could with chores and projects around the house. He would do them, and I would help. During my teen years, Dad was still able to outwork, outlift, and outperform me in most things.

As I entered my middle age years, it was almost a shock to see that role reversed. I guess we think our dads will always be… well, Dad. Soon I was doing the lion's share of the work, and he was helping. And that was OK. He was strong when I needed his strength, and now I needed to be strong because his strength had diminished.

Part of life is growing old. A part of living is dying. We all will reach a point where our strength fails, and we need to be cared for by our own the way we once cared for our own.

The Bible places the responsibility to care for our aged population upon their families — not upon the government, and not upon the church. As a son or daughter, you are responsible to care for your parents when the time comes when they cannot care for themselves. God says that if you fail in this responsibility, you are "worse than an infidel." An infidel is an unbeliever, an atheist, a person without faith or belief in God. Pretty serious!

Even though Jesus was dying on the cross, He took the time to see that His aged mother would be cared for. He would not be there to care for her personally, so He passed off that responsibility to a trusted disciple. What an example for all of us!

As you plan your future, and live out your life, keep in mind that there may come a time when you will need to — either financially or physically — care for your aged parents. Factor this into your life plan. This may, for a while, inconvenience your life. But remember — for several years, your mother's and father's lives were greatly inconvenienced to bear you, nurture you, provide for you, train you, and prepare you for life. It is only right that, if needed, you would be willing to pay that back.

Points to Ponder and Discuss:

1. What are some questions you should ask your mom about her past — about her life?

2. What are some questions you should ask your father about his past — about his life?

3. What are some specific things you can change that will improve the relationship that you have with your parents?

-8-

Your Relationship to Your Siblings

Lesson Goals:

1. To discover our responsibilities to our siblings.
2. To examine stories in the Bible that involve siblings so that we can learn Bible precepts that will help us.
3. To discover ways to be a blessing to our siblings.

Proverbs 17:17, *"A friend loveth at all times, and a brother is born for adversity."*

If you have brothers and sisters, you are blessed. At times, it may not seem so. Kids growing up under the same roof are provided ample opportunity for conflict. It is not always easy to get along, but the Bible teaches you that your sibling is the first person who will stand by you in times of adversity. A brother is born for that purpose! That is God's plan for siblings. Here are some Bible principles that will help you appreciate your siblings.

Bible Principles Concerning Your Siblings

There are many stories in the Bible that involve brothers and sisters. Here are some things you can learn from some of these stories.

1. Siblings may have the same parents, but each one is unique in his/her personality and interests.

Genesis 25:24-28, *"And when her days to be delivered were fulfilled, behold, there were twins in her* *womb. And the first came out red, all over like an hairy garment; and they called his name Esau. And after that came his brother out, and his hand took hold on Esau's heel; and his name was called Jacob: and Isaac was threescore years old when she bare them. And the boys grew: and Esau was a cunning hunter, a man of the field; and Jacob was a plain man, dwelling in tents."*

Esau and Jacob were twin brothers, yet different in so many ways. Obviously, these brothers were not identical twins because physically they were quite different. Also, their interests varied drastically. Esau was a "man of the field" and gained renown as a skillful hunter. Jacob was not as rugged, instead being more pious and studious. Esau loved the great outdoors and Jacob preferred to be inside. These marked differences seemed to fuel animosity between them. For whatever reason, it seemed that neither took the time to appreciate the strengths of the other.

Luke 10:38-42, *"Now it came to pass, as they went, that he entered into a certain village: and a certain woman named Martha received him into her house. And she had a sister called Mary, which also sat at Jesus' feet, and heard his word. But Martha was cumbered about much serving, and came to him, and said, Lord, dost thou not care that my sister hath left me to serve alone? bid her therefore that she help me. And Jesus answered and said unto her, Martha, Martha, thou art careful and troubled about many things: But one thing is needful: and Mary hath chosen that good part, which shall not be taken away from her."*

Mary and Martha were two sisters who possessed very different personalities. We see in this Bible story, that these differences produced conflict between the two. Martha received Jesus into her home. She wanted to make sure that her guests were properly cared for, so she was rushing about preparing food, drinks, and seeing to any other need that Jesus and his disciples might have. Mary on the other hand, looked at the opportunity differently. To Mary, this was an opportunity to sit and listen to the teachings of Christ and learn all she could from Him.

Martha was a server, conscious to see to the needs of those around her. Mary was more devotional, bent on seizing the opportunity for fellowship and interaction.

Martha became frustrated because Mary was not helping her serve the guests. Martha asked Jesus to rebuke her sister for what Martha perceived as laziness. Jesus took this moment to teach Martha a valuable lesson, and in doing so, to teach us all. Service is important – what Martha was doing was certainly admirable – but what Mary was doing was "needful." Serving God without taking time to fellowship with God has been the cause of many Christians "burning out" in the ministry. Duty needs devotion and devotion should produce duty.

The truth is, Mary could have learned from Martha, and Martha could have learned from Mary. All siblings can learn from each other. Consider these lessons:

1) Again, recognize that God made everyone in your family with different personalities and interests.

2) Do not criticize your brother or sister for being different from you. Being different does not equal being wrong. If we condemn everyone who is not the same as we are, then we imagine ourselves the standard of perfection. This attitude is prideful, not prudent.

3) Instead of letting differences create conflict, take the time to learn from each other. There is a balance in everything in life. Martha could have learned from Mary's devotion, while Mary, no doubt, could have gained by learning initiative from Martha.

4) Compliment the strengths of your siblings instead of criticizing their weaknesses. Anyone can find fault, but it takes a wise person to see the good in others.

5) Remember, it takes a lot of different personality types, character strengths, and skill sets to accomplish

the work of God. Every church needs a variety of people types. This should not be cause for conflict, but cause for celebration! Aren't you glad everyone is NOT like you! At the same time, be glad that there is a you. Find your place in your local church, and be thankful for every other person there.

2. Nothing produces conflict amongst siblings quite like the sins of jealousy and envy.

Genesis 37:1-11, *"And Jacob dwelt in the land wherein his father was a stranger, in the land of Canaan. These are the generations of Jacob. Joseph, being seventeen years old, was feeding the flock with his brethren; and the lad was with the sons of Bilhah, and with the sons of Zilpah, his father's wives: and Joseph brought unto his father their evil report. Now Israel loved Joseph more than all his children, because he was the son of his old age: and he made him a coat of many colours. And when his brethren saw that their father loved him more than all his brethren, they hated him, and could not speak peaceably unto him. And Joseph dreamed a dream, and he told it his brethren: and they hated him yet the more... And he dreamed yet another dream, and told it his brethren... And his brethren envied him..."*

Genesis 37:13-20, *"And Israel said unto Joseph, Do not thy brethren feed the flock in Shechem? come, and I will send thee unto them. And he said to him, Here am I. And he said to him, Go, I pray thee, see whether it be well with thy brethren, and well with the flocks; and bring me word again. So he sent him out of the vale of Hebron, and he came to Shechem... And when they saw him afar off, even before he came near unto them, they conspired against him to slay him. And they said one to another, Behold, this dreamer cometh. Come now therefore, and let us slay him, and cast him into some pit, and we will say, Some evil beast hath devoured him: and we shall see what will become of his dreams."*

Joseph's ten older brothers held animosity in their hearts against their younger brother. They were envious of him, and this envy soon turned to hatred. Why did they feel this way toward Joseph? What produced this strained relationship between them?

1) Joseph would not join in their evil doings. He even went a step beyond that and reported to their father the details of whatever evil they were involved in. One of the root causes of the animosity the older brothers felt toward Joseph boiled down to the fact that they wanted to do wrong, and he insisted on doing right.

This problem is as old as creation itself. Cain grew to hate his brother Abel, and that hatred caused him to commit the first murder. Why? Because Abel did right and Cain stubbornly insisted on doing wrong.

Genesis 4:1-9, *"And Adam knew Eve his wife; and she conceived, and bare Cain, and said, I have gotten a man from the LORD. And she again bare his brother Abel. And Abel was a keeper of sheep, but Cain was a tiller of the ground. And in process of time it came to pass, that Cain brought of the fruit of the ground an offering unto the LORD. And Abel, he also brought of the firstlings of his flock and of the fat thereof. And the LORD had respect unto Abel and to his offering: But unto Cain and to his offering he had not respect. And Cain was very wroth, and his countenance fell. And the LORD said unto Cain, Why art thou wroth? and why is thy countenance fallen? If thou doest well, shalt thou not be accepted? and if thou doest not well, sin lieth at the door. And unto thee shall be his desire, and thou shalt rule over him. And Cain talked with Abel his brother: and it came to pass, when they were in the field, that Cain rose up against Abel his brother, and slew him. And the LORD said unto Cain, Where is Abel thy brother? And he said, I know not: Am I my brother's keeper?"*

If you feel envy and jealousy toward one of your brothers or sisters, you need to be honest enough to examine your heart. Could the problem be that he or she wants to do right, and you insist on doing wrong? If so, the problem is not with them, it is with you. If you do not keep a right relationship with God, it will poison every other relationship in your life.

2) Joseph had a different mother. The Bible goes to lengths to point out that the seventeen-year-old Joseph was not just feeding the flocks with his brothers, but that he was with "the sons of Bilhah, and with the sons of Zilpah, his father's wives."

We live in a culture of blended families. These blended families sometimes are the result of the death of a parent, or the misfortune of a divorce between parents. One of the things young people in these situations need to guard against is animosity toward a half-brother or half-sister. Remember, neither of you chose your present situation. Ask God to give you a genuine love and appreciation for the family in which He has placed you.

3) Joseph's father loved him more than his older brothers. This is sad and unfortunate. No parent ought to have favorites. Israel (Jacob) made the same mistake that his father had made in rearing him and his brother.

Genesis 25:28, *"And Isaac loved Esau, because he did eat of his venison: but Rebekah loved Jacob."*

Sometimes a young person perceives favoritism. It is easy to get a martyr's mentality and decide that "Mom and Dad just love the other kids more than me." In most cases this is not true. In Joseph's case, it was. If you find yourself in this situation, do not become bitter against the favored child. He or she did not choose this situation either. I do think it might be wise to sit down with your parents and express how you feel about this. Of course, you should do so respectfully, but open communication about this might go a long way toward bringing unity again to your family.

Whatever the case may be, learn from it. If you are being reared in a home where there is favoritism, be sure that you do not do the same thing one day to your children.

4) Joseph was being prepared by God for a great purpose. There is no doubt that the dreams Joseph was having were divinely sent. We know this because of their prophetic accuracy. God was uniquely preparing Joseph for a supernatural purpose. From a young age, God's hand was upon him.

God calls from every generation young men for the ministry. He sanctifies some young ladies to be pastors' wives or missionaries' wives. This does not make you in any way superior to your siblings. A true call should produce humility in a young person, not pride. Notice the Apostle Paul's attitude:

Ephesians 3:8, *"Unto me, who am less than the least of all saints, is this grace given, that I should preach among the Gentiles the unsearchable riches of Christ."*

You may see God's calling come upon one of your brothers or sisters. Be glad for them! Encourage them to follow God's will for their lives no matter what it may be. Remember, no young person is a second-class Christian if God's plan for his life does not include full-time ministry. Don't let God's unique working in your brother or sister's life cause jealousy or envy to find a place in your heart.

3. Siblings can and should serve the Lord together!

John 1:40-42, *"One of the two which heard John speak, and followed him, was Andrew, Simon Peter's brother. He first findeth his own brother Simon, and saith unto him, We have found the Messias, which is, being interpreted, the Christ. And he brought him to Jesus."*

Matthew 4:18-22, *"And Jesus, walking by the sea of Galilee, saw two brethren, Simon called Peter, and An-*

drew his brother, casting a net into the sea: for they were fishers. And he saith unto them, Follow me, and I will make you fishers of men. And they straightway left their nets, and followed him. And going on from thence, he saw other two brethren, James the son of Zebedee, and John his brother, in a ship with Zebedee their father, mending their nets; and he called them. And they immediately left the ship and their father, and followed him."

Christ chose twelve disciples to personally train. Included in those twelve were two sets of brothers! It is the will of God that you and each of your siblings grow up to serve the Lord. If you get to do so in the same home church, or in the same ministry, you are doubly blessed!

It is also interesting that James — whom God used to pen the book of James — was the half-brother of Jesus Christ. Jude, another of Jesus' half-brothers, penned the book bearing his name. Family is important! It is the goal of every Christian mom and dad to live to see all of their children serving the Lord! Set this example for your siblings and encourage each other to this end.

Points to Ponder and Discuss:

1. Which Bible siblings did you most relate to?

2. What can you do specifically to help your brothers and sisters stay close to the Lord?

3. Is there something you need to make right with one of your siblings?

-9-

Your Relationship to Your Grandparents

Lesson Goals:

1. To discover our responsibilities to our grandparents.
2. To evaluate how successful we are in performing these responsibilities.
3. To be reminded of the blessings promised in the fulfilling of these responsibilities and the consequences attached to failing in these responsibilities.

Psalm 128:1-6, *"Blessed is every one that feareth the LORD; that walketh in his ways... Yea, thou shalt see thy children's children, and peace upon Israel."*

My grandparents had a profound influence upon my life. My dad's parents, Wilbur and Wilma Ross, were hard-working, gentle souls. They reared nine children, and possessed great character and integrity.

My mom's parents, Marvin and Ruth Ogle, were rugged, hard-working, opinionated, and delightful! All four grandparents survived the Great Depression and were a part of what has rightfully been labeled, "America's Greatest Generation." All four were dear to me.

The Grandparent/Grandchild Relationship

1. As a grandchild, you are a promised reward for your grandparents.

Psalm 128:5-6, *"The Lord shall bless thee....Yea, thou shalt see thy children's children..."*

It is hard for you as a grandchild to understand how precious you are to your grandparents. You are a blessing from the Lord. You are their second-chance children. You are their heritage.

I have marveled watching the sweetness of this relationship. It is a joy to experience it first-hand. A grandparent is unique in that most of us will be blessed to experience this relationship twice – once as the grandchild, and then as the grandparent. First you'll be the blessing – then one day you'll be the blessed!

2. Your grandparents wish to leave you an inheritance. Be wise enough to receive it.

Proverbs 13:22, *"A good man leaveth an inheritance to his children's children: and the wealth of the sinner is laid up for the just."*

1) Your grandparents carry the knowledge of three generations: theirs, their parents' and their grandparents'.

When you take the time to learn something from your grandparents, you very well may be learning something from your great, great grandparents. Generations overlap. Your grandparents' lives have been touched by every generation that preceded them. Now they are trying to pass all of that on to you. Don't drop the baton! If you fail to learn from them, you cannot pass their wisdom on to your future children and grandchildren.

Proverbs 30:11-13, *"There is a generation that curseth their father, and doth not bless their mother. There is a generation that are pure in their own eyes, and yet is not washed from their filthiness. There is a generation, O how lofty are their eyes! and their eyelids are lifted up."*

Don't be THAT generation. Be humble enough to sit at the feet of those who have come before you.

2) Your grandparents experienced, first-hand, the last 60 plus years of American history.

My mother was born in 1940. At the writing of this book, she is 78 years old. She has 12 grandchildren and over 30 great grandchildren. If our family is wise, we will take the time to talk to her about the America she knew. You can read about American History, and that is great! But how much better to talk to those who lived that history!

During my mother's first thirty years of life, she experienced these events:

1941 — Bombing of Pearl Harbor

1942-1945 — World War II

1943 — Race riots in Detroit and Harlem

1944 — Normandy Invasion, D-Day

1945 — Hitler and the Holocaust

1945 — Unconditional surrender of Germany

1945 — Franklin D. Roosevelt's sudden death; Vice President Harry S. Truman steps up

1945 — Two atomic bombs dropped on Japan; Japan surrenders

1946 — Philippines given independence by USA

1947 — Jackie Robinson breaks race barrier by becoming first black to play Major League Baseball

1949 — First round-the-world non-stop airplane flight

1950 -1953 — Korean War

1952 — First hydrogen bomb exploded

1953 — First color TVs go on sale

1954 — Brown vs Board of Education

1954 — Polo vaccine made available

1955 — Supreme court orders school integration

1956 — Interstate highway system initiated

1958 — First US satellite launched successfully

1959 — Both Alaska and Hawaii become states

1960 — John F. Kennedy becomes president

1961 — Bay of Pigs invasion of Cuba

1961 — First US manned space flight

1961 — Construction of the Berlin Wall begins

1962 — Cuban Missile Crisis

1963 — The Supreme Court of the United States ruled in the case of Abington School District vs. Schempp that laws requiring the recitation of prayer or Bible verses in public schools are unconstitutional

1963 — John F. Kennedy assassinated

1964 — Civil Rights Act passed by Congress

1964 — Vietnam War begins

1965 — Hippies, Draft Dodgers, Race Riots

1968 — Martin Luther King, Jr. assassinated

1969 — First man to land on the moon

This obviously is not an exhaustive list, but it is quite amazing what happened in America during just the first 30 years of my mother's life. How did these things affect her? How has America changed during her lifetime? Did any of her family serve in the military during any of these wars? Did they die for their country? How?

Your grandparents can teach you so much about history from their first person accounts of the events.

3) Your grandparents know details of your ancestry and of your heritage.

Your grandparents are also the guardians of your family history. Remember, they also personally knew and interacted with their parents, grandparents, and possibly great-grandparents. All of the personal stories of the previous generations will one day die with them if you don't take the time to sit and listen and record them.

In every family, there is the genealogy guru. This person has traced your family roots back for many generations. It grounds a person to know where they came from and who came before them. It also teaches you to number your days, and to be thankful for those who sacrificed much so that you can enjoy what you have today.

4) Your grandparents possess the wisdom of a lifetime of both good and bad decisions.

Your grandparents are not perfect. But remember, wisdom is gained not only by the good decisions of life, but also by the bad decisions. Listen to their advice and to their warnings. No one wants to see their grandchildren make the same mistakes they did.

Two questions that you may wish to ask your grandparents: What was the best decision you ever made? What was the worst?

5) Your grandparents will one day pass away, and when they do, everything they know will go with them.

Be thankful for every day God allows you to spend with your grandparents. There will probably be a day when you will attend their funeral. Hopefully, on that day, you can be glad that you received the things they were trying to pass down to you. If you did, you are rich, because you possess the knowledge, the understanding and the wisdom of your previous generations. Now you can pass these down to your children and grandchildren.

3. Decide on a list of questions that you will ask your grandparents.

Proverbs 18:4, *"The words of a man's mouth are as deep waters, and the wellspring of wisdom as a flowing brook."*

Proverbs 20:5, *"Counsel in the heart of man is like deep water; but a man of understanding will draw it out."*

The Bible speaks of counsel and wisdom as deep waters. In order to turn these wellsprings of wisdom into a flowing brook, you have to understand that it is your responsibility to "draw it out."

What I am saying is that most of what your grandparents know, they will only share if you take the time to show genuine interest. It is your responsibility to get it from them, not their responsibility to give it to you.

Matthew 7:7-8, *"Ask, and it shall be given you; seek, and ye shall find; knock, and it shall be opened unto you: For every one that asketh receiveth; and he that seeketh findeth; and to him that knocketh it shall be opened."*

I would encourage you to write out a list of questions to ask your grandparents. These questions could be about American history or family history. They could be questions about marriage, child rearing, finances or career advice. God has provided you people who are related to you who care about you and want to see you succeed in life. Tap into their wisdom.

Here are some possible questions to ask them:

What is your favorite childhood memory?

What is the best advice your father ever gave you?

What is the best advice your mother ever gave?

Where are your parents and grandparents buried?

How has America changed since you were a kid?

What was the saddest moment in your life?

What was the funniest thing that ever happened to you as a kid?

Why did your parents choose your name?

Who are some of the men or women you looked up to as heroes growing up?

How many brothers and sisters did you have? What was it like growing up during that time in history?

What advice would you give to me at my age?

Who were your grandparents (my great-great grandparents) and what are your memories of them?

Do you have a favorite Bible verse?

Where did you go to church as a child and which pastor had the biggest impact on you? Why?

Did you have animals as a kid? A favorite pet?

What jobs did you have as a teenager and as a young adult? How much did you make?

What was the first car you owned?

Did you serve in the military? What were your duties? What did you enjoy the most about it? Who else in our family served in the military?

These will get you started. As you listen to the stories that these questions unleash, you will think of other questions. Make notes as they answer, so you will remember the details later. It might be wise to keep a journal so that you can preserve your family history — not just for you to have, but for you to pass down to your children and grandchildren.

4. Your life should be a crown to your grandparents.

Proverbs 17:6, *"Children's children are the crown of old men; and the glory of children are their fathers."*

Remember, you are your grandparents' heritage. Your life should be lived in such a way that it brings honor upon your parents and grandparents.

Your have a responsibility to your family name. Your life, your actions and your treatment of others will either bring your family honor or dishonor. The Bible teaches us that a good name is important.

Proverbs 22:1, *"A good name is rather to be chosen than great riches, and loving favour rather than silver and gold."*

Ecclesiastes 7:1, *"A good name is better than precious ointment..."*

Sometimes I read the local paper, and see on the front page a picture of a young man or young woman who has been arrested for drunk driving, for using illegal drugs or for shop lifting. I always think of their grandparents — of the heartache and shame brought upon them by the foolish actions of a grandchild. Think before you act. Think about how it will reflect upon your family. Bring your grandparents honor by the way you live your life. Remember, you are their crown.

Points to Ponder and Discuss:

1. What do you know about your grandmother's life? What do you know about your grandfather's life?

2. What question would you like to ask your grandparents that is not listed in this chapter?

3. When were your grandparents born, and what event in history would you most like to ask them about?

-10-

Your Relationship to Your Pastor

Lesson Goals:

1. To discover our responsibilities to your pastor.
2. To evaluate how successful we are in performing these responsibilities.
3. To plan specifically how we can better encourage our pastor.

God, in His infinite wisdom, created the church and created the office of the pastor. God knew that every Christian needed a local assembly of believers to join himself to, and God knew that every believer needed a pastor. A pastor is a gift to the church, an under-shepherd to serve the Chief-shepherd by caring for His flock. The relationship between a Christian and his pastor is one of the sweetest and most sacred relationships available.

Ephesians 4:11-13, *"And he gave some, apostles; and some, prophets; and some, evangelists; and some, pastors and teachers; For the perfecting of the saints, for the work of the ministry, for the edifying of the body of Christ: Till we all come in the unity of the faith, and of the knowledge of the Son of God, unto a perfect man, unto the measure of the stature of the fulness of Christ:"*

Your pastor has been gifted to you by God to help bring you to Christian maturity. His goal is to use the Word of God to help you become Christ-like. He does this by way of teaching and preaching, edification, exhortation and rebuke. God gives your pastor a love for the people and a heart to see them be all that they can be for the Lord Jesus Christ. This is his responsibility, and he works diligently at it every week.

This is, however, not a one way relationship. You are assigned Biblical responsibilities when it comes to your pastor.

Responsibilities of a Teenager to His/Her Pastor

How can you be a blessing to your pastor? What are your responsibilities in this relationship?

1. Pray for your pastor.

1 Thessalonians 5:25, *"Brethren, pray for us."*

2 Thessalonians 3:1, *"Finally, brethren, pray for us, that the word of the Lord may have free course, and be glorified, even as it is with you:"*

Hebrews 13:18, *"Pray for us: for we trust we have a good conscience, in all things willing to live honestly."*

The apostles were used of God to jump-start the New Testament local church movement. They did so at great personal sacrifice — all eventually earning the martyr's crown. They asked one specific thing from those church members who benefited from their labors. That one thing was prayer. "Brethren, pray for us."

The most important thing you can do for your pastor is pray for him. Call out the name of your preacher before the throne of grace many times a day. Trust me, he faces attacks you will never face, he carries burdens you will never understand, and he must make decisions that you ought to thank the Lord you do not have to make. He needs your prayers.

1 Peter 5:1-8, *"The elders which are among you I exhort, who am also an elder, and a witness of the suffer-*

ings of Christ, and also a partaker of the glory that shall be revealed... Be sober, be vigilant; because your adversary the devil, as a roaring lion, walketh about, seeking whom he may devour:"

The warning concerning the roaring lion and his desire to devour is given in a portion of Scripture written specifically to pastors. Yes, the Devil would like to destroy the flock. But his best chance of scattering the flock is to attack the pastor. I share this with you because your pastor needs the protection that the prayers of his congregation provides. He needs his teenagers praying for him.

2. Remember your pastor and follow his faith.

Hebrews 13:7, *"Remember them which have the rule over you, who have spoken unto you the word of God: whose faith follow, considering the end of their conversation."*

The word "remember" in the above verse means "to be mindful of, to bring to recollection, to think of." The verse then goes on to remind you that God has set your pastor as the leader of your church, and that he is the one who teaches and preaches the Word of God to your congregation. The command to "remember" here is a reminder to all of the importance of your pastor's assigned position and the importance of his assigned duty.

Don't undervalue your pastor, and don't undervalue his preaching. Always respect his position and learn to appreciate the time he invests in studying and preparing his sermons.

Also, this verse commands you to follow the faith of your pastor. The word "faith" here speaks of religious or Scriptural truths. Don't just hear the messages he preaches, but let them affect your life. The Bible should change us. Bible preaching, properly received and applied, will make us more like Jesus.

These two commands to remember and follow are connected to the preaching of your pastor. Think about what he has preached, ponder it, meditate on it, then make definite decisions on how you will follow and obey the Bible principles he has presented.

A. W. Tozer wrote, "The true Church has never sounded out public expectations before launching her mission. Her leaders heard from God, they knew their Lord's will and did it. Their people followed them - sometimes to triumph, oftener to insults and public persecution - and their sufficient reward was the satisfaction of being right in a wrong world!"

3. Obey your pastor.

Hebrews 13:17, *"Obey them that have the rule over you, and submit yourselves: for they watch for your souls, as they that must give account, that they may do it with joy, and not with grief: for that is unprofitable for you."*

The next responsibility you have toward your pastor is to obey him. From time to time, God may lead your pastor to give you some specific Scriptural advice. He may see something in your life that you yourself may be blind to. Even if you don't understand or agree, if what he is asking you to do does not violate the Scriptures, submit yourself and follow his advice.

God has given your pastor the responsibility to watch for your soul. Your soul is one of three parts which together make up who you are — body, soul, spirit. Your soul is also a trinity and is made up of your mind, your heart and your will. Your pastor has been gifted to you to help you keep your soul right with God and right with God's Word.

How you *think* affects how you *feel.* How you *think* and *feel* will determine what you *decide* or what you *will.* If your pastor begins to see you making poor decisions, he understands that poor decisions are the result of wrong thinking. His job is to use the Word of God to help you think right. If you think Biblically about a situation, you will then feel correctly about it, and it will help you make the right decision.

Right Thinking + Right Emotions = Right Decisions

Be open to your pastor's counsel. Submit and yield to his Biblical advice. God has given him the duty of watching for your soul. If you respond with pride and rebellion to his attempts to help you, "that is unprofitable for you." And it brings grief to his heart.

4. Financially care for your pastor.

1 Corinthians 9:7-14, *"Who goeth a warfare any time at his own charges? who planteth a vineyard, and eateth not of the fruit thereof? or who feedeth a flock, and eateth not of the milk of the flock? Say I these things as a man? or saith not the law the same also? For it is written in the law of Moses, Thou shalt not muzzle the mouth of the ox that treadeth out the corn. Doth God take care for oxen? Or saith he it altogether for our sakes? For our sakes, no doubt, this is written: that he that ploweth should plow in hope; and that he that thresheth in hope should be partaker of his hope. If we have sown unto you spiritual things, is it a great thing if we shall reap your carnal things? If others be partakers of this power over you, are not we rather? Nevertheless we have not used this power; but suffer all things, lest we should hinder the gospel of Christ. Do ye not know that they which minister about holy things live of the things of the temple? and they which wait at the altar are partakers with the altar? Even so hath the Lord ordained that they which preach the gospel should live of the gospel."*

The Bible places the responsibility of the financial care of the pastor squarely on the shoulders of his congregation. Teenager, you are a member of that congregation. It is good to learn now, that, as a member of your church, you are to contribute to the care of your pastor.

The above portion of Scripture starts by asking some questions. When someone gives their life to join the army and protect their country, are they also expected to provide their own uniform, food, weapons, and armament? Or is that issued to them free of charge?

If someone exerts the labor and effort to plant a vineyard and tend to its care, is he wrong to partake of the fruit it produces?

If someone gives his life to the care and protection of a flock of sheep, is he wrong to partake of the milk that is produced from that flock?

The obvious answer to all three of these proposed examples is this: if a man is willing to give his life, offer his labor, stand guard and protect, then he certainly has earned the right to be taken care of by those he serves.

One of the reasons God commands us to place our tithes and offerings into the local assembly is for the care of the pastor and his family. God takes good care of the church who takes good care of His man. I have also watched God place a curse on congregations who begrudge the care of their pastor. If you are working a job, support your local assembly with your tithes and offerings.

5. Honor your pastor.

1 Timothy 5:17, *"Let the elders that rule well be counted worthy of double honour, especially they who labour in the word and doctrine."*

The word "honor" here means "value" — either concretely as in valuables or money, or by analogy as in dignity and esteem.

Since the verse calls for the church to reward those pastors who rule well (especially those who labor in word and doctrine) with double honor, it is proper to interpret the verse to include both meanings. A pastor should receive double honor — proper and generous financial care and proper and sincere respect and esteem.

Never be disrespectful to your pastor. Never tolerate the company of someone else who insists on being disrespectful toward him. Always call him by his proper title. A teenager should not call his pastor by his first name. Call him "Pastor", or "Preacher" or by the title Pastor followed by his last name.

A church (and/or your youth group) should plan ways to regularly show your pastor that you appreciate him and that you value him. How can you do this?

1) ***Your pastor feels valued when you want to spend time with him.*** Take time to speak with your pastor each week. Don't miss opportunities to spend time with him. If he plans something that he wants to do with the teens, be there.

2) ***Your pastor feels valued when you seek his opinion and his advice.*** Sit down with your pastor from time to time and let him know what is going on in your life. Ask him for advice when you are faced with decisions or difficulties.

3) ***Your pastor feels valued when you express appreciation for his work and his sacrifice.*** Thank him for his messages. Let him know you appreciate what he does for you and your family. From time to time, have the entire youth group plan something special for your pastor and his wife to let them know they are appreciated.

4) ***Your pastor feels valued when you express an appreciation for his preaching.*** He puts a tremendous amount of time and effort into his sermons. Sit up near the front, take notes, follow along in your Bible, and "Amen" what he preaches.

Charles Spurgeon said, “No music is more sweet to a gospel preacher than the rustle of Bible pages in the congregation.”

A teenager who recognizes the importance of having a good relationship with his pastor is wise beyond his years. Be a blessing to your pastor and God will bless you in return.

Points to Ponder and Discuss:

1. Why is it so important to pray for your pastor?

2. Explain the three parts of the soul and how those parts can work together in either a positive or negative way.

3. Come up with something you can do personally, or something your youth group can do collectively that would encourage your pastor and his wife.

-11-

Your Relationship to Your Friends

Lesson Goals:

1. To learn how to make friends.
2. To learn how to wisely choose our friends.
3. To learn what it means, according to God's Word, to be a friend.

Make Jesus Your Best Friend

One of the best pieces of advice I can give you as a young person is this: make Jesus your best friend. In chapter 3 of this book, we covered the Bible reasons why you should do this, and the Bible principles relating to how to do this. Whether you realize it or not, you do not have a better friend. He has proven His love to you by dying for you. This is the greatest proof of a true friend.

John 15:13, *"Greater love hath no man than this, that a man lay down his life for his friends."*

John 15:15, *"Henceforth I call you not servants; for the servant knoweth not what his lord doeth: but I have called you friends; for all things that I have heard of my Father I have made known unto you."*

Once you have decided that Jesus will be your best friend, let Him exercise veto power in the choosing of all of your other friends. He will not steer you wrong!

Charles Spurgeon wrote, "The good man has his enemies. He would not be like his Lord if he had not. If we were without enemies we might fear that we were not the friends of God, for the friendship of the world is enmity to God."

Be Careful in Choosing Your Friends

Proverbs 13:20, *"He that walketh with wise men shall be wise: but a companion of fools shall be destroyed."*

This verse contains both a promise and a warning. If you choose wise friends, you will continue to increase in wisdom. If you choose the companionship of fools, their influence will at some point destroy you. Show me your friends today and I will tell you what you will become tomorrow.

Proverbs 1:5, *"A wise man will hear, and will increase learning; and a man of understanding shall attain unto wise counsels:"*

Proverbs 1:7, *"The fear of the LORD is the beginning of knowledge: but fools despise wisdom and instruction."*

The wise man in Proverbs is defined as someone who responds positively to both instruction and reproof. The foolish man is described as one who despises instruction and refuses reproof. Watch how your peers react to those in authority over them. The young man or young lady who has become scornful of their parents, rebellious toward their teachers and pastor is — according to God's Word — a fool. Stay away from them. Do not let them have influence in your life.

If you have already built friendships with foolish young people, you need to begin to distance yourself from those influences. I know this can be hard, but remember the "shall be" in Proverbs 13:20. As much as you may care about them or want to help them, you cannot change a Bible principle. Many good young people have been destroyed because they refused to dissolve close friendships with those given over to foolishness.

Look for that young person who has the right attitude toward instruction and reproof. Watch to see if they obey their parents and respect their pastor. Watch how they respond to Bible preaching. When they need to be rebuked, how do they handle it? A young person who responds wisely to these situations will make a good friend for you.

Understanding How to Gain Friends

Proverbs 18:24, *"A man that hath friends must shew himself friendly: and there is a friend that sticketh closer than a brother."*

Many young people carry a bitterness in their heart because they feel that they do not have any friends. Some find it hard to make friends. Sadly, others have been so desperate to have a friend that they have built friendships with the wrong crowd. We have covered how to choose the right kind of friend, but how do you begin to build a friend relationship?

First, learn to be comfortable alone. You can only do this when you realize, as a Christian, you are not alone. Remember, the best friend you can have is Jesus. If that is the only friend you ever have, you are still blessed.

Secondly, consider the friendships available to you offered by those outside your age group. Sadly, many young people are locked into the mentality that a real friend must be someone close to their own age. As a teenager, you should begin to build a friendship with your parents and your grandparents. Find people older than you in your church who are the type of person you wish to emulate, then ask to spend some time with them. As a teenager, some of my closest friends were older men who took the time to teach me the things I needed to learn.

Also, consider building friendships with those younger than yourself. You can be a great role model to older elementary students and, if you are in high school, to those in junior high.

Lastly, consider young people of your age group who display a desire to do right. How are these friendships birthed? You gain friends by showing yourself friendly. Most young people are insecure. It seems everyone is waiting for someone to reach out to them. As a Christian, we need to learn to be the ones who reach out.

Learn to smile at people. Don't be afraid to go over and introduce yourself to someone you don't know. Ask questions about their family, their hobbies, and their interests. See if you can find something that you have in common, and build on that. If you have nothing in common, ask them to explain something that they are interested in that you know nothing about. Let them teach you about it.

If you meet someone new at church, ask them to sit with you. Compliment their clothes, hairstyle, or shoes. If they are not very talkative, then you do the talking. If they are talkative, you do the listening. Always steer the conversation away from negativity and toward something positive. Be excited about what is going on at your church and your opportunities to serve the Lord.

Be friendly to everyone, but choose your friends carefully. George Washington is credited with this quote, "It is far better to be alone than in bad company."

R. A. Torrey wrote, "I would rather go to Heaven alone than go to Hell in company."

Three Principles of a Biblical Friendship

A biblical friendship can be a blessing to both people involved. There are three Bible principles that define a profitable friendship.

1. Don't forsake a friend in time of need.

Proverbs 17:17, *"A friend loveth at all times, and a brother is born for adversity."*

Proverbs 27:10, *"Thine own friend, and thy father's friend, forsake not; neither go into thy brother's house in the day of thy calamity: for better is a neighbour that is near than a brother far off."*

Maybe you have heard the phrase, "fair-weather friend." All of us will go through the storms of life, but during those times, you will find out who your friends really are. People will always remember who stood beside them and helped them in their "day of calamity." Learn to be there for people when they need a friend the most.

The Bible not only encourages us to stand by our friends, but it also adds, "and thy father's friend, forsake not". My dad is now in Heaven. He was a Baptist preacher for over 40 years. During that time, there were some men who stood by my dad — true friends who supported him. I make a point to maintain close friendships with those men. If they need me, I'm there. I do this because of what they meant to my father, and because of what my father meant to them.

2. A true friend will tell you the truth, even if it hurts.

Proverbs 27:5-6, *"Open rebuke is better than secret love. Faithful are the wounds of a friend; but the kisses of an enemy are deceitful."*

A real friend will be honest with you — even when the truth hurts. He will tell you what you need to hear, even if it is not what you want to hear.

Be careful. Many young people have wrecked their lives because of the deceitful "kisses of an enemy." If someone agrees with you when you are wrong, covers for you when you do wrong, or joins you in doing wrong, they are not your friend, they are an enemy. It may not seem like it at the time, but when you wreck your life, you will look back and realize that those who helped you do it were certainly not your friends.

Thomas Fuller prayed, "God send me a friend that will tell me of my faults."

3. A true friend will challenge you to be your best.

Proverbs 27:17, *"Iron sharpeneth iron; so a man sharpeneth the countenance of his friend."*

A true measure of a friend is this: when you spend time with them you come away better for it. A real friend will sharpen you, not dull you. They will challenge you to be a better Christian and a better person.

When I look at these three principles of a true friend, I am again reminded that Jesus is the best friend I have ever had. He has never forsaken me. He has always been there in the toughest times of my life. Jesus, Who is the Word, has always been truthful with me, even when the truth hurts. The time I spend with Him always makes me better.

Strive to be that kind of a friend to others, and God will send people into your life who will be that kind of a friend to you.

Points to Ponder and Discuss:

1. Why is Jesus the best friend any of us could have?

2. When you consider the Bible principles of a true friend, who has been that person in your life?

3. Is there someone who you thought was a friend, but the Word of God has shown you that they are not a true, biblical friend? What should you do about it?

-12-

Your Relationship to the Lost

Lesson Goals:

1. To understand the debt we owe every lost person.

2. To understand what it is to be ready to share the Gospel with the lost.

3. To determine to not be ashamed of the Gospel of Jesus Christ.

No one came into this world a Christian. We all were born with the curse of sin upon us. If you are saved today, it is because God used someone to share the Gospel with you. God used someone — maybe many "someones" — to help get you to Jesus.

I was born to parents who were not Christians. When I was five, we moved to Brazil, Indiana. God saw to it that the neighbors across the road from us were faithful Christians. Jerry and Ruth Purcell began to invite our family to church. Eventually we went, and Pastor Elmer Evans faithfully preached the Gospel to us. His wife, Vietta Evans, taught me in Sunday School. She was gifted at taking the Bible and teaching it so that children could understand what Jesus had done for them. Our entire family found Christ at the small country Baptist church. God saved us, but He used many people there to welcome us, love us, pray for us, witness to us, and teach and preach to us.

I owe them. And I pay them back by paying it forward. Pass on what was given to you.

"I Am Debtor"

Romans 1:14, *"I am debtor both to the Greeks, and to the Barbarians; both to the wise, and to the unwise."*

Remember, we define our relationships by our responsibilities. What is my responsibility to those without Christ as their Savior? I owe them what was given to me. I owe them the Gospel.

Paul recognized this concept as he penned the words, "I am debtor." He spent his life paying back those who influenced him for Christ by becoming one of the greatest soul winners of the early church movement.

Honest men and women pay their debts. It is dishonest for a born-again Christian not to be busy sharing the Gospel of Jesus Christ with those who are lost. You make a payment on that debt every time you hand out a gospel tract, share your salvation testimony, or attend your church's weekly outreach program. You are not responsible for what a man does with the Gospel once he has received it, but you are responsible to see that he receives it.

"I Am Ready"

Romans 1:15, *"So, as much as in me is, I am ready to preach the gospel to you that are at Rome also."*

In order to pay that debt, we must be prepared. Paul wrote, "I am debtor," then right afterwards, "I am ready!" God used Paul in a mighty way, because he was always ready to be used.

When I was in Bible college, I was blessed to have many opportunities to preach. One of my friends asked me one day, "Jerry, why is it that you get to preach all the time and others of us are seldom asked?" I answered, "If a faculty member walked up to you right now and asked if you could grab your Bible, come with him, and preach at the Rescue Mission, what would you say?"

My friend pondered, then answered, "I'd have to tell him that I couldn't. I'd need time to go and prepare a message."

I smiled. "That's why they come and ask me. I'm always ready."

God is going to open up soul winning opportunities to those who have taken the time to prepare. How can you be always ready to share the Gospel?

1) Take a good soul winning course. Every church should regularly offer a soul winning training course to its members. This course will train you how to open up your Bible and explain to someone who is lost how they can be saved.

Philip was led by the Spirit of God into the desert to meet a man who was sitting in his chariot reading the Scriptures. This man was a man of great influence, but he was without Christ.

Acts 8:30-35, *"And Philip ran thither to him, and heard him read the prophet Esaias, and said, Understandest thou what thou readest? And he said, How can I, except some man should guide me? And he desired Philip that he would come up and sit with him.... Then Philip opened his mouth, and began at the same scripture, and preached unto him Jesus."*

If God gave you a similar opportunity, would you be ready? Would you be prepared to open the Bible and explain to someone how they can be saved? This is of utmost importance! Not every teenager will be called of God to be a preacher, an evangelist, or a missionary, but every teenager can and should be a soul winner.

2) Carry with you a New Testament. I always have a New Testament close by. Carry one on your person when possible. Have one in every vehicle, in your lunch pail, your tool bag, or whatever you carry to your place of employment.

3) Carry gospel tracts. You will not always have an opportunity or the time to get into a lengthy discussion with someone about eternity, but you can offer to them a pamphlet that explains the Gospel of Jesus Christ.

4) Prepare your heart. Don't leave your house each morning before spending time with the Lord. Stay in the Word of God. Pray each morning and ask the Lord to lead you to someone who needs Jesus.

In 1936, Will H. Houghton wrote the words to a beautiful chorus that we would be blessed to learn and blessed to sing as we start each day.

Lead me to some soul today,
O teach me, Lord, just what to say;
Friends of mine are lost in sin,
And cannot find their way.
Few there are who seem to care,
And few there are who pray;
Melt my heart, and fill my life,
Give me one soul today.

5) Prepare your eyes. Be looking, always looking for an opportunity. Don't get so busy trying to accomplish your "to-do list" that you race past people who are in need. I call this being "soul-conscious."

Jesus is our ultimate example when it comes to noticing people that others ignored or overlooked. Jesus heard the voice of blind Bartimaeus while others rebuked his cries. Jesus saw the need of a woman drawing well water while others could only think of her checkered past. While others scurried under a sycamore tree, Jesus took the time to see who was up in it. When His disciples tried to turn the children away, Jesus stepped in and took them into His arms and blessed them.

There are people all around us. Start seeing them.

"I Am Not Ashamed"

Romans 1:16, *"For I am not ashamed of the gospel of Christ: for it is the power of God unto salvation to every one that believeth; to the Jew first, and also to the Greek."*

Are you ashamed of Jesus? Are you ashamed of being a Christian? What is preventing you from becoming a bold witness for Jesus Christ? Here are three ways to increase your boldness.

1) Purge your life of sinful, wicked habits.

Proverbs 28:1, *"The wicked flee when no man pursueth: but the righteous is bold as a lion."*

Unconfessed, habitual sin will make any Christian a coward. Don't be a stranger to the church altar. Stay right with God. Stay right with your parents. Stay right with those around you. Confession provides us with forgiveness and cleansing; it also provides us with the courage of a lion.

2) Read often all four accounts of the crucifixion of Christ.

John 19:38, *"And after this Joseph of Arimathaea, being a disciple of Jesus, but secretly for fear of the Jews, besought Pilate, that he might take away the body of Jesus..."*

Mark 15:43, *"Joseph of Arimathaea... went in boldly unto Pilate, and craved the body of Jesus."*

Joseph of Arimathaea was a secret disciple. He chose to live out his faith quietly and privately because he was afraid of the repercussions from those around him. Now, he "comes out of the closet" so to speak. What caused him to make this decision? He watched the Son of God die on the cross. After watching what Jesus was willing to suffer on Calvary for him, he was convicted over his lack of boldness. He then publicly associated with Christ.

Make yourself an eyewitness to what transpired on Golgotha's hill, and do it often. Watching the courage with which Jesus gave His life for us cannot help but give us the courage to be willing to give our lives for Him.

3) Refuse to live your life fearing men, but instead choose to dedicate your life to God.

Hebrews 13:6, *"The Lord is my helper, and I will not fear what man shall do unto me."*

Philippians 1:20, *"According to my earnest expectation and my hope, that in nothing I shall be ashamed, but that with all boldness, as always, so now also Christ shall be magnified in my body, whether it be by life, or by death."*

At some point, you must start being ashamed of being ashamed of Jesus! Kneel before the cross and forever pledge your allegiance to the One who was willing to give His life for you.

Every member of the body of Christ owes the Gospel to the lost. Ask God to give you the courage to pay your debt. Then speak up boldly for Christ!

Points to Ponder and Discuss

1. What is the difference between being separated from the world and being isolated from the lost?
2. Make a list of people you know that need the Lord Jesus Christ as their Savior, and begin to pray for them to be saved. Then write beside their names what you can do to get them the Gospel.
3. Answer honestly this question: What is keeping me from being a bolder witness for Jesus?

-13-

Your Relationship to Your Neighbors

Lesson Goals:

1. To help us understand our responsibilities to those who live around us.
2. To help us see our neighborhood as a mission field.
3. To help us to become good neighbors.

The Bible has much to teach us about this important relationship — that of being a good neighbor. Let's see what the Book of Proverbs will teach us about our responsibilities in this important relationship.

What Makes Us a Good Neighbor?

1. Understand the value of having neighbors.

Proverbs 14:21, *"He that despiseth his neighbour sinneth: but he that hath mercy on the poor, happy is he."*

Proverbs 11:2, *"He that is void of wisdom despiseth his neighbour: but a man of understanding holdeth his peace."*

The word "despiseth" means to "undervalue." It means to fail to place the proper importance upon someone or something. Some Christians see absolutely no value and no responsibility to those who live around them. God warns us that this attitude is both foolish and sinful.

It ought to be very important to those of us who are saved to be good neighbors. You cannot claim to be a good Christian while being a bad neighbor. Let's take this relationship seriously.

2. View your neighborhood as a mission field.

Mark 5:18-19, *"And when he was come into the ship, he that had been possessed with the devil prayed him that he might be with him. Howbeit Jesus suffered him not, but saith unto him, Go home to thy friends, and tell them how great things the Lord hath done for thee, and hath had compassion on thee."*

Jesus commanded this new convert to "go home" and share his story with those friends who lived around him. We should all take this as a personal challenge.

I mentioned in the last chapter that God used our next door neighbors to invite my then unsaved parents to church. It was because of their concern for my family that my dad and mom eventually became Christians. I have often wondered how different my life might have been if they had not seen their neighborhood as a mission field.

I do not believe in coincidences. I believe that I live where I do for a reason. In 1994, the Lord allowed my wife and me to purchase a home just north of Jasonville, Indiana. We immediately set out to befriend those who lived around us. In the years since, we have been able to see some of them accept Jesus as their Savior.

3. Do not talk evil of your neighbors.

Proverbs 11:9, *"An hypocrite with his mouth destroyeth his neighbour: but through knowledge shall the just be delivered."*

God says you are a hypocrite if you use your mouth to destroy the reputation of your neighbor. I realize that there are some people who live around you who are not good neighbors, but there is no good reason to talk them down to others, If you do, you will sacrifice the opportunity to exercise influence in their lives. You can malign them, and what you say may even be true, but by doing so you may forfeit the chance to see them saved.

One of the wisest things to assume in life is this: whatever you say about someone will eventually get back to that someone. People talk. Sadly, the average person is more excited about sharing something negative than sharing something positive.

Colossians 4:5-6, *"Walk in wisdom toward them that are without, redeeming the time. Let your speech be alway with grace, seasoned with salt, that ye may know how ye ought to answer every man."*

4. Personally go to your neighbors to work out differences.

Proverbs 25:9, *"Debate thy cause with thy neighbour himself; and discover not a secret to another:"*

Shortly after we purchased our property back in 1994, I decided to get a couple of puppies for our girls. We lived in the country and owned over 8 acres of property, so our new pets had plenty of room to romp. Puppies don't stay puppies, and as they grew, they decided to become more and more adventuresome. One morning I walked out of my front door, and there, lying by the step, was a well-chewed work boot — and it didn't belong to me! During the night, the little thieves had visited one of our neighbors, and stole a new chew-toy from off of his back step.

After giving both dogs a good scolding, and chaining them up, I then picked up the boot and got in the truck to go door to door apologizing. I finally found which neighbor the boot belonged to and gave the man the money he needed to buy a new pair of work boots. He didn't have to come looking for me, I went to him.

If you have an issue with one of your neighbors, go and talk it over with him. Don't complain to the other neighbors, go to him. If you go with the right spirit, you can usually work things out between the two of you.

5. Provide security for your neighbors.

Proverbs 3:29, *"Devise not evil against thy neighbour, seeing he dwelleth securely by thee."*

Growing up, I remember that my Dad would go across the road and tell the Purcells when we would be gone for a few days. He did this because he knew they were Christians and he knew they would keep an eye on our place while we were gone. They would always inform us when they left on a vacation also.

Sadly, that has changed in today's society. Most people are scared for their neighbors to know when they are gone.

Your neighbors ought to be glad that you live near them. Neighbors ought to watch out for one another, not seek opportunity to take advantage of each other.

The neighbor that lives across from us has cattle. I also raise a few head of beef myself. From time to time, cows get out of their fenced area. I have helped him chase his cows back in, and he has helped me chase mine! That's what neighbors do for one another.

6. Go out of your way to befriend and help poor neighbors.

Proverbs 3:28, *"Say not unto thy neighbour, Go, and come again, and to morrow I will give; when thou hast it by thee."*

Proverbs 14:20-21, *"The poor is hated even of his own neighbour: but the rich hath many friends. He that despiseth his neighbour sinneth: but he that hath mercy on the poor, happy is he."*

Proverbs 14:31, *"He that oppresseth the poor reproacheth his Maker: but he that honoureth him hath mercy on the poor."*

Find ways to be a special blessing to poor neighbors. Go out of your way to be kind to them. Don't look down your nose at anyone because their clothes are not as expensive as yours, or their house not as nice. God is no respecter of persons. This means He loves everyone the same. Often, the world will belittle and make fun of the poor. As a Christian, we should do just the opposite.

Also, take special consideration for widows who live around you. Go out of your way to help elderly neighbors. God will bless you for being especially kind to senior citizens.

7. Do not covet anything that is your neighbor's.

Exodus 20:17, *"Thou shalt not covet thy neighbour's house, thou shalt not covet thy neighbour's wife, nor his manservant, nor his maidservant, nor his ox, nor his ass, nor any thing that is thy neighbour's."*

God instructs us how to treat people who have less than us, but what about those who have more than us? It is just as wrong to envy the well-to-do as it is to despise the poor.

One of the Ten Commandments warns us against covetousness. A person who is always trying to "keep up with the Joneses" will often make foolish financial decisions in his life. There are always going to be those who have more than you do. Remember — the most important things in life are not *things*. Be thankful for what you have, and be glad for those who have more, but do not give in to jealousy, envy and covetousness.

8. Be friendly, but not intrusive, with your neighbors.

Proverbs 25:17, *"Withdraw thy foot from thy neighbour's house; lest he be weary of thee, and so hate thee."*

Part of being a good neighbor is respecting the privacy of those around you. There is a fine line between being friendly and being a nuisance. Understand that people are busy, and when they finally get home, they usually want to get some projects done or just relax awhile.

If you do go over for a visit, don't overstay your welcome. Be friendly, be brief, and be welcome the next time. This is much better than being bothersome, burdensome, and marked as one to be avoided!

Henry Ward Beecher said, "There's not much practical Christianity in the man who lives on better terms with angels and seraphs, than with his children, servants and neighbors."

The Bible has much to say about being a good neighbor. Let's ask God to help us improve these important relationships.

Points to Ponder and Discuss:

1. Which neighbor did God bring to your mind as you read this chapter? Specifically, what did God tell you to do?
2. How can you be a better neighbor to a widow or elderly couple who lives near you?
3. Who has been a good neighbor to your family? What makes them so?

-14-

Your Relationship to Your Future Spouse

Lesson Goals:

1. To identify our responsibilities to our future spouse.
2. To understand that the success or failure of this future relationship will be largely determined BEFORE this relationship begins.
3. To emphasize the importance of prayer, preparation, purity and patience in the life of a young person.

For most of you reading this book, God's will is for you one day to be married. Sometime in the future, you will be blessed to be a part of a relationship that takes two people and makes them one. Except for your relationship with God, this should be the sweetest, most intimate of all relationships. This is one you want to get right!

In order for that to happen, you must start now. You must embrace now the responsibilities that will make this future relationship blessed. Before you ever meet the one God has created for you to marry, you should determine to do some things for him/her NOW.

1. You have the responsibility to pray for him/her.

You might be thinking, "But I don't even know who he/she is!"

No you don't, but God does. If you really believe that God has created someone for you, then somewhere on this planet he/she now exists. He/she woke up this morning, and is now living out this day. You will someday share your life with this person. Why should it seem strange for you to pray for God to bless his/her day, for God to protect him/her, and for God to keep him/her close to Him?

Long before I knew her, while still a teenager, I began to pray for my future wife. I believe that may have been one of the reasons I knew her when I met her. Call it strange if you want, but God heard my prayers, protected my future wife, and in His time, brought us together.

After you are married, will you pray for your wife or husband every day? Then why wait? Start today.

2. You have the responsibility to prepare for him/her.

Sadly, too many Christian young people spend their teenage years pursuing a boyfriend or girlfriend instead of preparing for the future husband or wife that God has for them. Trust the Lord! He will bring you to the one He has for you in His time.

Until then, don't waste your youth on pursuing relationships that God never intended you to have. Instead of pursuing, spend your time preparing.

As a young man, you need to be prepared to one day be the leader your wife needs you to be. Before you can lead anyone, you have to be willing to first follow. Are you surrendered to the Lord's will in your life? Are you willing to be directed by the Word of God?

Secondly, a young man must be prepared to leave. When an immature young man talks of leaving home, he often uses the word, "freedom."

"I can't wait to be able to move out and have my freedom!" Son, let me educate you. The word "freedom" is spelled r-e-s-p-o-n-s-i-b-i-l-i-t-y. Forming a new family unit is a great responsibility!

Matthew 19:4-5, *"...For this cause shall a man leave father and mother, and shall cleave to his wife: and they twain shall be one flesh?"*

Freedom? Yes, you will have the "freedom" to mentally, physically, emotionally, financially, and spiritually lead and support a new family unit. You will have the "freedom" to work long, hard hours, to pay your own bills, the "freedom" to overcome financial setbacks, face and solve your marriage problems, fix your own car when it breaks down, pay medical and dental bills for your family and deal with the ever-changing stages of your children as they grow and develop. Welcome to freedom!

As a young lady, you too need to be busy preparing for your future husband. If he is prepared to lead, are you prepared to follow? Will you be an asset to your husband as you become his help meet? Are you ready to take on the day to day management of a new home? Are you now developing the skill sets that will allow you to be successful in running a happy, efficient, cost-effective, God-centered home?

Are you preparing or are you wasting your teenage years pursuing dead-end relationships and participating in activities that do nothing to ready you for real life?

3. You have the responsibility to remain pure for him/her.

The modern day culture is lying to young people. It promotes promiscuity and scoffs at purity. Yet God's Word has not changed. Purity is still important and fornication is still condemned.

I Thessalonians 4:3, *"For this is the will of God, even your sanctification, that ye should abstain from fornication:"*

Don't let Satan deceive you. Not everyone is "doing it." Multitudes of Christian young people across America are preserving their purity as a gift that they will someday give to the one God has created for them.

4. You have the responsibility to wait for him/her.

Genesis 2:22, *"And the rib, which the LORD God had taken from man, made he a woman, and brought her unto the man."*

God has made someone for you. Just as God brought Eve to Adam when the time was right, God will lead you to the one He has for you — in HIS time. Till then, like Adam, go to sleep in this area of your life.

Be patient. The Devil will try to pawn off his counterfeits on you before God brings you the right one. Stay in God's will. Listen to wise and godly counsellors. Involve your parents in the process. And did I mention to be patient? :) You never have to break a Bible principle to find God's perfect will.

Points to Ponder and Discuss:

1. Can what you do during your teenage years adversely affect your future marriage? How?
2. What are some things you can do now to make sure you are properly prepared to succeed in your future marriage relationship?
3. Are you trusting God in this area of your life? Or do you feel that you have to make it happen?

-15-

Forbidden Relationships

Lesson Goals:

1. To examine a list of people with whom God says it is not wise to develop a close relationship.
2. To examine the whys behind these forbidden relationships.
3. To determine to trust God's Word by obeying the cautions it contains.

"No one has a right to pick my friends but me!"

This came out of the mouth of a very angry fifteen -year-old young lady (accompanied by the stomping of her foot for emphasis!). My answer?

"No one? Not even God?"

That was fifteen years ago. Not surprisingly, her life as a thirty-year-old is a train wreck. Teenagers who decide that they are wiser than the Scriptures are doomed to find out how foolish they really are. How about you? If God says that certain relationships are off limits, do you take it as a dare? Or are you wise enough to understand that God is trying to protect you?

Forbidden Relationships

1. A Romantic Relationship with an Unbeliever

II Corinthians 6:14, *"Be ye not unequally yoked together with unbelievers: for what fellowship hath right-*

eousness with unrighteousness? and what communion hath light with darkness?"

Salvation changes you. When you got saved, you became a child of God and a new creature in Jesus Christ. No matter how much you have convinced yourself how much you and an unsaved person have in common, in the deepest and most fundamental way, you are incompatible.

Determine to obey the Lord in this area of your life. Only consider a romantic relationship with someone who both professes to be saved, and lives a life that backs up that profession.

2. A Companionship with a Foolish Person

Proverbs 13:20, *"He that walketh with wise men shall be wise: but a companion of fools shall be destroyed."*

Every Christian young person would be wise to do a study on the foolish man of the book of Proverbs. This study will help you identify a foolish person both by what he says and what he does.

Don't be too quick to judge. All of us, at some time or another, have acted foolishly. But a person whose life bears the constant evidences of a fool should be avoided.

One man once said, "Show me your friends today, and I'll show you who you will be tomorrow." God not only warns of the contagiousness of foolishness, but goes on to warn of the danger of companioning with fools. Walk with wise men and women. Avoid the foolish. Trust God on this and you will be glad you did.

3. A Friendship with an Angry Person

Proverbs 21:19, *"It is better to dwell in the wilderness, than with a contentious and an angry woman."*

Proverbs 22:24, *"Make no friendship with an angry man; and with a furious man thou shalt not go:"*

Proverbs 29:22, *"An angry man stirreth up strife, and a furious man aboundeth in transgression."*

A young lady graduated from our Christian school years ago. She began pursuing a young man who had a notorious temper. Despite the warning of her parents and many of her friends, she married this young man. Three years later, they held her funeral. Shortly after she married this hot-head, he began to verbally abuse her. Sadly, soon his temper caused him to cross the line to physical abuse — and then to murder.

I know men who spend their lives walking on eggshells because they made the mistake of marrying a woman with a bad temper. Son, I don't care how pretty she is! You don't want to spend your life living with that.

The Bible is plain — "make no friendship!" Your life will be strife-filled if you disobey this exhortation.

4. An Association with Someone Who is Living in Open, Unrepentant Sin

Psalms 1:1, *"Blessed is the man that walketh not in the counsel of the ungodly, nor standeth in the way of sinners, nor sitteth in the seat of the scornful."*

Avoid people who are ungodly, who live in open sin, and who are scornful of righteousness and godliness. If you do not, the Bible warns that you will forfeit God's blessings upon your life. Disobedience to Psalms 1:1 is the number one reason that young people end up out of God's will.

George Washington once said, "Associate yourself with men of good quality if you esteem your own reputation. It is better be alone than in bad company."

5. A Relationship with Someone Involved in Sexual Sins

I Corinthians 5:9, *"I wrote unto you in an epistle not to company with fornicators:"*

Proverbs 29:3, *"Whoso loveth wisdom rejoiceth his father: but he that keepeth company with harlots spendeth his substance."*

Trust the Lord in this area of your life. If one of your dearest friends begins to live a life that involves any habitual sexual sin, then dissolve that friendship immediately. Make no exception to this rule.

This does not mean you cannot pray for them, but to keep company with them is to disobey a direct command of God. The more exposed to these sins you are, the less offensive they can become. The next thing you know, you find yourself committing these sins.

6. The Company of an Enticer

Proverbs 1:10-16, *"My son, if sinners entice thee, consent thou not. If they say, Come with us, let us lay wait for blood, let us lurk privily for the innocent without cause: Let us swallow them up alive as the grave; and whole, as those that go down into the pit: We shall find all precious substance, we shall fill our houses with spoil: Cast in thy lot among us; let us all have one purse: My son, walk not thou in the way with them; refrain thy foot from their path: For their feet run to evil, and make haste to shed blood."*

Colossians 2:4, *"And this I say, lest any man should beguile you with enticing words."* An enticer is any person who uses words to encourage and tempt you to join them in doing wrong.

The word found in the Hebrew that is translated "entice" means "to make roomy" or "to open" or "enlarge". The enticer encourages you to be more "open minded", to make room in your mind to at least consider the possibility of a wrong action. They help "enlarge" your desire and make the possibility more alluring and appealing. They are the persuasive, deceptive voice that tells you that it is OK – to go ahead and give in to what you know in your heart is displeasing to God.

In short, an enticer is someone who is a bad influence. Ask the Holy Spirit to help you examine those who are close to you, as we study the enticer.

An enticer will entice secretly. They will wait till you are away from your parents and your pastor to approach you. Many enticers are using technology to send their enticing words to you. They will try to drive a wedge between you and the God-given authority in your life. If you have to keep any conversation or communication secret from your parents and pastor, that should tell you it is wrong.

Deuteronomy 13:6-8, *"If thy brother, the son of thy mother, or thy son, or thy daughter, or the wife of thy bosom, or thy friend, which is as thine own soul, entice thee secretly, saying, Let us go and serve other gods, which thou hast not known, thou, nor thy fathers... thou shalt not consent unto him, nor hearken unto him; neither shall thine eye pity him, neither shalt thou spare, neither shalt thou conceal him:"*

How should you react to an enticer?

1) Say no! Loud and clear.

2) Get away from him or her.

3) Expose them to someone in authority. If you fail to do this last one, you allow them to continue on to another potential victim. Do not pity an enticer! Do not worry about being called a tattle-tale or a rat. Those are intimidation tactics an enticer uses so that he can remain unexposed and continue his sinful mission.

7. A Friendship with a Scorner

Proverbs 19:25, *"Smite a scorner, and the simple will beware: and reprove one that hath understanding, and he will understand knowledge."*

Proverbs 22:10, *"Cast out the scorner, and contention shall go out; yea, strife and reproach shall cease."*

Proverbs 24:9, *"The thought of foolishness is sin: and the scorner is an abomination to men."*

A scorner is one who publicly holds a teaching authority (both the message and the messenger) in derision; one who vocally scoffs, vocally mocks, vocally imitates in mockery a parent, a teacher or a preacher; one who mocks truth.

This would be the young person (or God forbid, the adult) who sits beside you in church and whispers snide remarks during a sermon. Or the friend who openly mocks the rules and advice of his parents. A scorner will openly challenge, with looks and lip, the Sunday School teacher or school teacher.

When a person becomes this bold in their mockery and defiance of those in authority over them, the Bible says all that is left is to smite them (verbally) and cast them out. No one in authority ought to put up with a scorner. God says they are an abomination to men.

How foolish to become a scorner! Perhaps the only thing more foolish is to keep company with one.

Points to Ponder and Discuss:

1. Is there a relationship in your life that you need to dissolve?
2. Are you a good influence to those around you?
3. Review all seven of these forbidden relationships. How should you react to each?

-16-

Iron Sharpening Iron

Proverbs 27:17, *"Iron sharpeneth iron; so a man sharpeneth the countenance of his friend."*

I collect knives. I sincerely believe a man can never have too many knives or too many guns. My wife does not agree — she thinks I need therapy! I think I just need one more knife.

If you are going to keep your knife sharp, you have to use sharpening steel. Metal on metal produces the sharpest edge. It also produces friction and heat. It also grinds off of the knife blade anything that is keeping it dull. The process is tedious, but the result is worth it.

The people in your life who will help you become your best for the Lord are not always the ones with whom you would prefer to spend time. Our carnal nature wants to be coddled and congratulated, not corrected and challenged. The wisest young people purposefully choose to spend time with people who will challenge them to be all that they can be for the Lord Jesus Christ.

It is well worth your time to invest in healthy relationships. Remember, a successful relationship requires you fulfilling your responsibilities. Proper relationships will help draw you closer to God and will make you want to be a better person. Let the right kind of people help prepare you. Embrace proper relationships and avoid forbidden relationships.

After all, you can't sharpen a knife on a marshmallow!

About the Author

Jerry Ross is the pastor of the Blessed Hope Baptist Church in Jasonville, Indiana. He and his wife, Sheryl, have served the Lord together for over 35 years. In addition to pastoring, Pastor Ross is a popular teen speaker, Bible conference speaker, and author.

"A Teenager's Guide" Series

Now available….

A Teenager's Guide to Character, Success and Happiness

A Teenager's Guide to the Invisible Creation

A Teenager's Guide to Healthy Relationships

Coming soon….

A Teenager's Guide to the Local New Testament Church

A Teenager's Guide to Victorious Christian Thinking

A Teenager's Guide to Self-Discipline and Organization

A Teenager's Guide to Silent Killers and Besetting Sins

A Teenager's Guide to the Holy Bible and Prevailing Prayer

A Teenager's Guide to First Century Christianity

A Teenager's Guide to End-Time Prophecy

Order by Phone: (812) 665-4375

Order On-Line: www.stayinthecastle.com

Other Books by the Author

Seven Royal Laws of Courtship
The Teenage Years of Jesus Christ
The Childhood Years of Jesus Christ
The 21 Tenets of Biblical Femininity
The 21 Tenets of Biblical Masculinity
Is Your Youth Group Dead or Alive?
Mountain Lessons
Grace Will Lead Me Home
104 Teen Bible Lessons
Did God Put a Book Inside of You?

Stay in the Castle Series

Stay in the Castle
The Warrior Prince
The Chosen One
The Prodigals

The Teenager's Guide Series

A Teenager's Guide to Character, Success, & Happiness
A Teenager's Guide to the Invisible Creation
A Teenager's Guide to Healthy Relationships